LIBRA PATH
YOUR DAILY 2025 HOROSCOPE GUIDE

AMANDA M CLARKE

Welcome to The Libra Path: Your Daily 2025 Horoscope Guide. This book is designed to provide Libra readers with daily astrological insights, offering guidance, inspiration, and cosmic wisdom for each day of the year. Whether you're seeking clarity on relationships, career, or personal balance, these horoscopes will help you navigate the year ahead with mindfulness and grace. Use this guide to reflect, set positive intentions, and align with the universe's energy as you journey through 2025, walking your unique path with harmony and purpose.

Copyright © 2024 by Koru Lifestylist

All rights reserved. All content, materials, and intellectual property in this book or any other platform owned by Koru Lifestylist are protected by copyright laws. This includes text, images, graphics, videos, audio, software, and any other form of content that may be produced by Koru Lifestylist.

No part of this content may be reproduced, distributed, or transmitted in any form or by any means without the prior written permission of Koru Lifestylist. This means that you cannot copy, reproduce, or use any of the content in this book for commercial or personal purposes without the express written consent of Koru Lifestylist.

Unauthorized use of any copyrighted material owned by Koru Lifestylist may result in legal action being taken against you. Koru Lifestylist reserves the right to pursue all available legal remedies against any individual or entity found to be infringing on its copyright.

In summary, Koru Lifestylist © 2024 holds exclusive rights to all the content produced by it, and any unauthorized use of such content will result in legal action.

Disclaimer: The Libra Path: Your daily 2025 horoscope guide book provides information on astrological readings and intuitive interpretations, it is not intended as a substitute for professional advice, diagnosis, or treatment. The information contained in this book is provided for educational and entertainment purposes only and is not meant to be taken as specific advice for individual circumstances. The author and publisher make no representations or warranties with respect to the accuracy or completeness of the contents of this book and specifically disclaim any implied warranties of merchantability or fitness for a particular purpose. The reader should always consult with a licensed professional for any specific concerns or questions. The author and publisher shall not be liable for any loss or damage caused or alleged to have been caused, directly or indirectly, by the information contained in this book. The use of this book is at the reader's sole risk

LIBRA
Libra: September 23 – October 22

2025 Overview

Libra in 2025 Overview

Libra, 2025 is a year of balance, growth, and self-discovery for you. You'll feel an increased focus on both relationships and personal development, with opportunities to realign with your true desires. The year encourages you to evaluate your career, connections, and lifestyle, making thoughtful adjustments for long-term happiness and success. Your natural diplomacy will shine as you navigate challenges with grace, creating harmony in both personal and professional spheres.

Expect breakthroughs in your career, where hard work is recognized and rewarded. Relationships deepen, offering emotional fulfillment and stronger bonds. Embrace change, trust your instincts, and maintain balance—2025 will be a year of personal empowerment, harmony, and growth.

Libra in 2025
Love and Relationships

Libra, in 2025, love and relationships will take on new depth and meaning. This year, you'll focus on strengthening your emotional connections and creating harmony within your partnerships. Whether in romantic relationships, friendships, or family ties, communication and understanding will be key to fostering deeper bonds.

For those in committed relationships, expect moments of renewal and growth as you and your partner work through challenges with grace and empathy. Single Libras may find meaningful connections that align with their values and desires.

2025 is a year of healing and emotional fulfillment—allow yourself to trust, love deeply, and embrace the journey ahead.

Libra in 2025
Career

In 2025, Libra, your career takes center stage with exciting opportunities for growth and advancement. This year encourages you to step into leadership roles, showcase your skills, and pursue long-term career goals. Your natural diplomacy and ability to balance perspectives will make you a valuable asset in the workplace, leading to recognition and success.

Expect breakthroughs as your hard work is rewarded with promotions or new responsibilities. If you're considering a career change, 2025 is a favorable time to explore new paths that align with your passions. Stay organized, trust your instincts, and maintain a healthy work-life balance for sustained success.

Libra in 2025
Wealth

In 2025, Libra, your financial landscape is set for stability and growth, but it will require careful planning and mindful decision-making. This is the year to take control of your wealth by reviewing your budget, savings, and investments. Your natural sense of balance will help you make practical financial choices, ensuring long-term security.

Opportunities to increase your income may arise, whether through a promotion, new job, or smart investments. However, avoid impulsive spending and focus on building a solid financial foundation. By staying disciplined and thoughtful with your money, you'll find yourself in a stronger, more prosperous position by year's end.

Libra in 2025
Health

In 2025, Libra, prioritizing your health and wellbeing will be essential to maintaining balance in all areas of your life. This year encourages you to focus on both physical and mental health, ensuring that you create habits that support your overall vitality. Regular exercise, a balanced diet, and mindfulness practices like meditation or yoga will keep you grounded and energized.

Stress management will be key, especially with increased responsibilities in other areas of life. Take time to rest and recharge, listen to your body's needs, and avoid overextending yourself. By nurturing your health, you'll maintain the harmony you thrive on throughout 2025.

Libra in 2025
Study

In 2025, Libra, your intellectual curiosity will be sparked, making this a great year for study and personal development. Whether you're returning to formal education, pursuing a new skill, or deepening your knowledge in a particular field, this year will present opportunities for learning and growth.

You'll thrive in structured environments, where discipline and focus will help you absorb new information quickly. Stay organized and create a study plan that works for you, balancing learning with rest. Embrace challenges as they come, and trust that expanding your mind will lead to personal and professional growth, enriching your future.

*To my lovely Libra friend
Jo-Ann Wallington*

*Your grace, kindness, and gentle spirit
have always been a source of calm and
positivity.
This book is dedicated to you, with
appreciation for the balance and
beauty you bring into the world.*

*May 2025 be filled with harmony, joy,
and all the wonderful things you
deserve*

LIBRA
DAILY HOROSCOPE

2025

January 2025

Libra

01-January-2025

Today, dear Libra, the new year invites you to seek balance between personal aspirations and professional responsibilities. Embrace changes with an open heart, for they will lead to personal growth. Reflect on what you truly value and take steps toward enhancing your wellbeing. Surround yourself with people who support your vision, and let go of those who hinder your progress. Focus on self-love today.

Affirmation & Gratitude

"I trust the journey and embrace the balance between my dreams and responsibilities."

Libra

02-January-2025

Today, dear Libra, creative energies flow freely, inspiring you to embark on new projects. Trust your instincts and lean into your artistic passions. Collaborating with like-minded people will bring success, so don't shy away from teamwork. Let your imagination lead the way, and don't hesitate to express your uniqueness.

Affirmation & Gratitude

"I embrace my creativity and welcome collaboration to enhance my vision."

Libra

03-January-2025

Today, dear Libra, communication is key. Conversations that you've been avoiding can now be approached with diplomacy and clarity. Listen deeply and speak with intention. Relationships, both personal and professional, benefit from transparency. Take time to reassess your connections and express gratitude for the positive ones.

Affirmation & Gratitude

"I communicate clearly and compassionately, fostering harmony in all my relationships."

Libra

04-January-2025

Today, dear Libra, balance your work and personal life. You may feel torn between various obligations, but taking time for self-care will restore your inner peace. Prioritize your wellbeing today, and don't hesitate to set boundaries where needed.

Affirmation & Gratitude

"I honor my need for balance and make space for rest and self-care."

Libra
05-January-2025

Today, dear Libra, your intuition is heightened. Trust the subtle messages the universe is sending your way. Tune into your inner voice, and let it guide you in decision-making. Meditation or a quiet moment alone may bring clarity on an important matter.

Affirmation & Gratitude

"I trust my intuition and listen to the wisdom within me."

Libra

06-January-2025

Today, dear Libra, focus on nurturing relationships. A heart-to-heart conversation with someone close may deepen your bond. Your ability to empathize and provide support shines today. Reach out and make time for meaningful connections, but also ensure you're being nurtured in return.

Affirmation & Gratitude

"I nurture my relationships with love, compassion, and understanding."

Libra

07-January-2025

Today, dear Libra, your analytical skills come to the forefront. Tackle tasks that require focus and attention to detail. Take a step back from the emotional and look at things objectively. This is a good day for planning, organizing, and getting things in order.

Affirmation & Gratitude

"I approach challenges with clarity and organize my path to success."

Libra

08-January-2025

Today, dear Libra, new opportunities for growth and learning may appear. Be open to expanding your knowledge or skills, as this can propel you forward in unexpected ways. Don't be afraid to step out of your comfort zone and embrace change.

Affirmation & Gratitude

"I welcome new opportunities for growth and courageously step out of my comfort zone."

Libra

09-January-2025

Today, dear Libra, there may be moments of indecision, but trust that everything will fall into place. Weigh your options carefully without overthinking. Lean on your support system for advice, but ultimately, follow what feels right for you.

Affirmation & Gratitude

"I trust myself to make the right decisions and honor my inner guidance."

Libra
10-January-2025

Today, dear Libra, it's time to focus on your health and wellbeing. Pay attention to both physical and mental balance. Small changes in your daily routine can have significant benefits, so consider integrating healthier habits.

Affirmation & Gratitude

"I honor my body and mind by nurturing them with care and attention."

Libra
11-January-2025

Today, dear Libra, creative ideas are abundant. Let your imagination run wild, and take this opportunity to dive into artistic pursuits. Whether it's painting, writing, or designing, expressing your creativity today will bring you joy and fulfillment.

Affirmation & Gratitude

"I celebrate the beauty of creativity and let my imagination flow freely."

Libra
12-January-2025

Today, dear Libra, your diplomatic nature will serve you well in resolving a conflict. Approach sensitive situations with calm and understanding. Seek compromise, and you'll find the peace you're looking for in both personal and professional areas.

Affirmation & Gratitude

"I approach conflict with a calm heart and seek peaceful resolutions."

Libra

13-January-2025

Today, dear Libra, focus on practical matters. You may need to reassess your finances or organize your schedule. Use this day to plan for the future and create a solid foundation for what lies ahead.

Affirmation & Gratitude

"I create stability in my life by planning with care and foresight."

Libra

14-January-2025

Today, dear Libra, your social side is activated. Enjoy moments with friends and family, and let your charming personality shine. This is a great day for networking or simply sharing joyful moments with loved ones.

Affirmation & Gratitude

"I cherish my connections and radiate positivity in all my interactions."

Libra
15-January-2025

Today, dear Libra, a spiritual journey may call to you. Take time to reflect on your inner world, and consider engaging in meditation or other practices that connect you to your higher self. The universe has wisdom to share if you're willing to listen.

Affirmation & Gratitude

"I embrace my spiritual journey and open myself to the wisdom of the universe."

Libra
16-January-2025

Today, dear Libra, your sense of justice and fairness is strong. You may be called to stand up for someone or something you believe in. Use your voice to promote equality and fairness, but remember to keep balance in mind.

Affirmation & Gratitude

"I stand up for fairness and use my voice to bring harmony into the world."

Libra
17-January-2025

Today, dear Libra, it's a good time to focus on self-expression. You have a lot to say, and your words hold power. Whether through writing, speaking, or artistic endeavors, express yourself with confidence and authenticity.

Affirmation & Gratitude

"I express myself with confidence and allow my true voice to shine through."

Libra
18-January-2025

Today, dear Libra, expect an unexpected twist. The day may bring some surprises, so remain flexible and open to change. Trust that whatever comes your way is meant to shift you in a positive direction.

Affirmation & Gratitude

"I embrace the unexpected and trust that the universe is guiding me toward growth."

Libra

19-January-2025

Today, dear Libra, it's important to take a break from the hustle. Rest and recharge, and allow yourself to relax without feeling guilty. Reflect on all you've accomplished and be kind to yourself.

Affirmation & Gratitude

"I give myself permission to rest and recharge, knowing I deserve it."

Libra

20-January-2025

Today, dear Libra, your leadership qualities shine. You may be called to take charge in a group setting or project. Lead with confidence, but also listen to the opinions of others to foster a collaborative environment.

Affirmation & Gratitude

"I lead with confidence, while embracing the strength of teamwork and collaboration."

Libra
21-January-2025

Today, dear Libra, balance is key. You may find yourself juggling multiple responsibilities. Stay organized, and ensure you're making time for both work and play. Remember that you can't pour from an empty cup, so prioritize your wellbeing.

Affirmation & Gratitude

"I find balance in my life and ensure that I take time for both work and rest."

Libra

22-January-2025

Today, dear Libra, a wave of nostalgia may wash over you. Embrace it and take time to reconnect with old friends or revisit past memories. There's wisdom in reflecting on your past, but ensure you stay grounded in the present.

Affirmation & Gratitude

"I honor my past while staying fully present in the beauty of the now."

Libra

23-January-2025

Today, dear Libra, you may feel a pull toward helping others. Whether through charity or lending a hand to a friend, your generous spirit shines bright. Remember to balance your giving nature with receiving love and support in return.

Affirmation & Gratitude

"I give with an open heart and allow myself to receive the support I deserve."

Libra

24-January-2025

Today, dear Libra, focus on your goals and aspirations. It's a great day to reassess your long-term plans and make adjustments if needed. Stay motivated and trust that the universe will support your ambitions.

Affirmation & Gratitude

"I stay focused on my goals and trust that the universe is aligning in my favor."

Libra

25-January-2025

Today, dear Libra, adventure calls! Step out of your comfort zone and explore new places, ideas, or experiences. Embrace the unknown, as it brings exciting opportunities for growth and fun.

Affirmation & Gratitude

"I welcome new experiences and embrace adventure with an open heart."

Libra

26-January-2025

Today, dear Libra, self-care is essential. You've been giving a lot of yourself lately, and now it's time to refill your cup. Pamper yourself with a peaceful day of rest and relaxation.

Affirmation & Gratitude

"I prioritize self-care and nurture my body, mind, and spirit."

Libra

27-January-2025

Today, dear Libra, financial matters may require your attention. Take a closer look at your budget or investments, and make necessary adjustments. Practical steps taken today can bring long-term stability.

Affirmation & Gratitude

"I make wise financial choices that lead to long-term security and abundance."

Libra

28-January-2025

Today, dear Libra, relationships are in focus. Strengthen bonds with loved ones by being present and attentive. Small gestures of kindness will go a long way in creating harmony and connection.

Affirmation & Gratitude

"I nurture my relationships with love, presence, and appreciation."

Libra

29-January-2025

Today, dear Libra, creativity is once again on the rise. Use this energy to brainstorm new ideas or pursue a passion project. Don't be afraid to think outside the box.

Affirmation & Gratitude

"I embrace my creative spirit and allow my imagination to take flight."

Libra

30-January-2025

Today, dear Libra, emotions may run high. Allow yourself to feel deeply, but try not to get overwhelmed. Ground yourself through meditation or a walk in nature, and let your emotions flow naturally.

Affirmation & Gratitude

"I allow my emotions to flow freely, knowing they are a vital part of my human experience."

Libra

31-January-2025

Today, dear Libra, it's time to celebrate your accomplishments. Whether big or small, take a moment to recognize how far you've come. You've worked hard, and now it's time to enjoy the fruits of your labor.

Affirmation & Gratitude

"I celebrate my achievements and acknowledge the progress I've made on my journey."

February 2025

Libra

01-February-2025

Today, dear Libra, focus on teamwork. Collaborating with others will bring fresh perspectives and help you accomplish your goals. Be open to new ideas and appreciate the unique talents of those around you.

Affirmation & Gratitude

"I embrace collaboration, knowing that together we achieve greater things."

Libra
02-February-2025

Today, dear Libra, a deep sense of compassion fills your heart. You may be called to offer support or advice to a loved one. Listen with empathy, and trust your natural ability to bring peace and comfort to those in need.

Affirmation & Gratitude

"I offer compassion and support, knowing that kindness strengthens my bonds with others."

Libra

03-February-2025

Today, dear Libra, focus on your home environment. Organizing your space or making small improvements can bring harmony to your surroundings. A peaceful, tidy home will boost your mental clarity and productivity.

Affirmation & Gratitude

"I create harmony in my life by nurturing the space around me."

Libra
04-February-2025

Today, dear Libra, a moment of reflection is needed. Take a step back from the hustle and tune into your inner thoughts. Meditate, journal, or simply enjoy some quiet time to process your emotions and gain clarity on your next steps.

Affirmation & Gratitude

"I take time to reflect and listen to the wisdom within me."

Libra

05-February-2025

Today, dear Libra, your social charm is irresistible. It's an excellent day to connect with friends or network in professional settings. Your natural charisma opens doors and forges meaningful connections, so put yourself out there and enjoy the interactions.

Affirmation & Gratitude

"I connect with others with joy and positivity, knowing that my presence brings light."

Libra

06-February-2025

Today, dear Libra, focus on your career ambitions. You may find yourself at a crossroads, and it's time to make decisions that align with your long-term goals. Trust your instincts and take the bold steps necessary to move forward.

Affirmation & Gratitude

"I trust my vision for the future and confidently make decisions that support my growth."

Libra
07-February-2025

Today, dear Libra, unexpected surprises may arise. Stay flexible and embrace the changes with an open heart. Remember that sometimes the universe shifts things around for your benefit, even if it feels unsettling at first.

Affirmation & Gratitude

"I welcome unexpected changes, trusting that they lead me toward greater possibilities."

Libra
08-February-2025

Today, dear Libra, emotions run high, but your ability to maintain balance will keep things in check. Be mindful of your reactions and seek peaceful resolutions in any conflicts that arise. Your calm demeanor will inspire those around you.

Affirmation & Gratitude

"I remain calm and balanced in the face of emotional challenges."

Libra
09-February-2025

Today, dear Libra, focus on intellectual growth. It's a great day for learning, whether it's reading, taking a class, or diving into a new subject. Stimulating your mind will bring new insights and help you expand your horizons.

Affirmation & Gratitude

"I embrace the opportunity to learn and grow, expanding my knowledge and wisdom."

Libra
10-February-2025

Today, dear Libra, relationships take center stage. Whether romantic or platonic, take time to deepen your connections with others. Small acts of kindness and thoughtful communication will strengthen bonds and bring joy into your life.

Affirmation & Gratitude

"I nurture my relationships with love, trust, and open communication."

Libra

11-February-2025

Today, dear Libra, financial matters may require your attention. Reevaluate your budget or long-term plans, and make any necessary adjustments. Practical decisions made today can set the foundation for future security.

Affirmation & Gratitude

"I make wise financial choices that support my stability and abundance."

Libra
12-February-2025

Today, dear Libra, you may feel pulled between conflicting responsibilities. Stay organized and don't be afraid to delegate tasks where necessary. Prioritizing your time wisely will help you maintain balance and avoid burnout.

Affirmation & Gratitude

"I prioritize my responsibilities with clarity and allow myself to ask for help when needed."

Libra
13-February-2025

Today, dear Libra, take a moment to celebrate the little things in life. Gratitude is a powerful tool, and by appreciating what you have, you'll attract more positivity into your world.

Affirmation & Gratitude

"I am grateful for the blessings in my life, big and small."

Libra
14-February-2025

Today, dear Libra, love is in the air. Whether you're in a relationship or focusing on self-love, take time to celebrate your heart. Romantic gestures, thoughtful moments, or simple self-care will fill your day with warmth and joy.

Affirmation & Gratitude

"I open my heart to love, embracing the beauty of connection and kindness."

Libra
15-February-2025

Today, dear Libra, your focus shifts to personal growth. Consider areas of your life where you wish to improve, and set realistic goals to move forward. The steps you take today will lead to long-term fulfillment.

Affirmation & Gratitude

"I take positive steps toward personal growth, knowing that each effort brings me closer to my best self."

Libra
16-February-2025

Today, dear Libra, trust your instincts. An opportunity may present itself, and your gut feeling will guide you in the right direction. Don't second-guess yourself—your intuition is strong, and the universe supports your choices.

Affirmation & Gratitude

"I trust my intuition and confidently follow the guidance of my inner wisdom."

Libra
17-February-2025

Today, dear Libra, focus on physical health. Whether it's exercise, a healthy meal, or simply taking a walk in nature, give your body the attention it deserves. Taking care of your physical wellbeing will enhance your overall happiness.

Affirmation & Gratitude

"I honor my body with love and care, nurturing it with healthy habits."

Libra
18-February-2025

Today, dear Libra, emotions may be intense, but don't shy away from them. Allow yourself to feel deeply and process your emotions in a healthy way. It's okay to be vulnerable, as it brings healing and growth.

Affirmation & Gratitude

"I embrace my emotions and allow them to guide me toward healing and growth."

Libra
19-February-2025

Today, dear Libra, focus on your creative side. Whether it's art, music, writing, or any other form of expression, channel your inner artist. Let your creativity flow freely, without judgment or hesitation.

Affirmation & Gratitude

"I celebrate the beauty of creativity and express myself with joy and freedom."

Libra
20-February-2025

Today, dear Libra, balance is key. You may feel pulled in different directions, but remember that balance comes from within. Prioritize your needs and set boundaries where necessary to protect your peace.

Affirmation & Gratitude

"I create balance in my life by honoring my needs and setting healthy boundaries."

Libra

21-February-2025

Today, dear Libra, a sense of adventure calls to you. Whether it's exploring a new place or trying something different, step outside of your routine. Embrace spontaneity and see where it leads.

Affirmation & Gratitude

"I welcome adventure and embrace new experiences with an open heart."

Libra

22-February-2025

Today, dear Libra, focus on spiritual growth. Meditate, connect with nature, or engage in practices that nourish your soul. Reflect on your inner journey and consider how you can deepen your spiritual connection.

Affirmation & Gratitude

"I honor my spiritual path and open myself to deeper wisdom and understanding."

Libra

23-February-2025

Today, dear Libra, challenges may arise, but remember that you are resilient. Approach any difficulties with grace and determination, knowing that you have the strength to overcome them.

Affirmation & Gratitude

"I face challenges with courage and grace, trusting in my resilience."

Libra

24-February-2025

Today, dear Libra, focus on your long-term goals. Take time to reflect on where you want to be in the future and make a plan to get there. Small steps taken today will lead to great success down the road.

Affirmation & Gratitude

"I plan for my future with confidence, knowing that each step brings me closer to my dreams."

Libra

25-February-2025

Today, dear Libra, your social nature is highlighted. Reach out to friends or loved ones and enjoy meaningful connections. Laughter and lighthearted conversations will brighten your day and strengthen your relationships.

Affirmation & Gratitude

"I cherish my friendships and enjoy the joy and connection they bring into my life."

Libra

26-February-2025

Today, dear Libra, focus on self-care. You've been giving a lot of yourself lately, and now it's time to recharge. Take a break, pamper yourself, and prioritize your wellbeing.

Affirmation & Gratitude

"I take time for myself, knowing that rest and self-care are essential to my wellbeing."

Libra

27-February-2025

Today, dear Libra, new opportunities may present themselves. Stay open to possibilities and don't be afraid to take a leap of faith. Trust that the universe is aligning things in your favor.

Affirmation & Gratitude

"I embrace new opportunities with confidence, trusting that the universe supports my path."

Libra
28-February-2025

Today, dear Libra, focus on gratitude. Take time to reflect on all the things you're thankful for, and share your appreciation with those around you. Gratitude will bring even more abundance into your life.

Affirmation & Gratitude

"I am grateful for the blessings in my life, and I share my appreciation with an open heart."

March
2025

Libra
01-March-2025

Today, dear Libra, focus on financial stability. Reassess your budget, investments, and long-term goals. Practical choices made now will bring future abundance. Stay grounded and think wisely before making any big decisions.

Affirmation & Gratitude

"I make wise financial decisions that support my long-term stability and abundance."

Libra

02-March-2025

Today, dear Libra, relationships are at the forefront. Nurture the important connections in your life by offering love and support. Deep, meaningful conversations will strengthen bonds and bring you closer to those you care about.

Affirmation & Gratitude

"I nurture my relationships with love, compassion, and understanding, deepening the bonds I share with others."

Libra

03-March-2025

Today, dear Libra, a sense of adventure fills the air. It's a great day to break away from routine and try something new. Explore new hobbies, visit new places, or meet new people. Embrace the joy of spontaneity.

Affirmation & Gratitude

"I welcome new adventures and experiences with excitement and an open heart."

Libra
04-March-2025

Today, dear Libra, focus on your wellbeing. Pay attention to both your mental and physical health. Engage in self-care activities that nourish you from within, and don't hesitate to take time for yourself.

Affirmation & Gratitude

"I honor my body, mind, and spirit by nurturing them with love and care."

Libra

05-March-2025

Today, dear Libra, communication flows smoothly. Use this opportunity to express yourself clearly, whether in personal or professional settings. Honest conversations will help resolve lingering issues and create harmony.

Affirmation & Gratitude

"I communicate with clarity and honesty, creating harmony in all my relationships."

Libra
06-March-2025

Today, dear Libra, creative energy is high. Channel your imagination into projects that inspire you. Whether it's art, writing, or problem-solving, let your creativity shine and don't be afraid to think outside the box.

Affirmation & Gratitude

"I embrace my creativity and let my imagination flow freely."

Libra
07-March-2025

Today, dear Libra, your diplomatic skills will be tested. A conflict may arise, but you have the ability to bring balance and peace to the situation. Approach any disputes with calm and understanding, and seek compromise where possible.

Affirmation & Gratitude

"I resolve conflicts with calm and balance, bringing peace and understanding to every situation."

Libra

08-March-2025

Today, dear Libra, focus on long-term goals. Take a step back to reassess your plans and make adjustments where necessary. Small changes now will create a clearer path for future success. Stay patient and trust the process.

Affirmation & Gratitude

"I trust the journey toward my goals, knowing that each step brings me closer to success."

Libra
09-March-2025

Today, dear Libra, your social charm is in full effect. It's a perfect day to connect with friends, network, or meet new people. Your positive energy will attract good vibes, and you'll leave a lasting impression on those you encounter.

Affirmation & Gratitude

"I radiate positive energy, attracting joyful and meaningful connections into my life."

Libra
10-March-2025

Today, dear Libra, emotions may run high. Take time to ground yourself and process your feelings before reacting. This is a day for introspection and self-awareness, so give yourself space to reflect and grow.

Affirmation & Gratitude

"I embrace my emotions with kindness, allowing them to guide me toward healing and growth."

Libra
11-March-2025

Today, dear Libra, focus on personal growth. It's a great day to engage in learning or self-improvement. Whether you take up a new skill or dive deeper into personal development, trust that the effort you invest in yourself will pay off.

Affirmation & Gratitude

"I embrace opportunities for growth and learning, knowing they bring me closer to my best self."

Libra
12-March-2025

Today, dear Libra, love is in the air. Whether you're in a relationship or practicing self-love, take time to nurture your heart. Acts of kindness, romance, or simply appreciating yourself will bring warmth and joy into your day.

Affirmation & Gratitude

"I open my heart to love, kindness, and connection, embracing the beauty of every moment."

Libra

13-March-2025

Today, dear Libra, your analytical side comes to the forefront. Use this day to tackle tasks that require focus and attention to detail. Your ability to think critically will help you solve problems and make sound decisions.

Affirmation & Gratitude

"I approach challenges with clarity and precision, trusting my ability to find the best solutions."

Libra
14-March-2025

Today, dear Libra, your leadership skills shine. You may be called to take charge of a situation or guide others. Lead with confidence and compassion, and remember that collaboration is key to achieving success.

Affirmation & Gratitude

"I lead with confidence and compassion, knowing that teamwork brings greater results."

Libra
15-March-2025

Today, dear Libra, adventure calls. Break free from your routine and explore something new. Whether it's a trip, a hobby, or a new experience, embrace the unknown and let your curiosity guide you.

Affirmation & Gratitude

"I embrace the excitement of new experiences and open myself to adventure with joy."

Libra
16-March-2025

Today, dear Libra, focus on balance. You may feel pulled in different directions, but remember to prioritize what matters most. Set boundaries where needed and take time for self-care to maintain inner harmony.

Affirmation & Gratitude

"I create balance in my life by setting healthy boundaries and prioritizing my wellbeing."

Libra
17-March-2025

Today, dear Libra, focus on gratitude. Take a moment to appreciate the blessings in your life, both big and small. A grateful heart attracts more abundance, so share your appreciation with the universe and those around you.

Affirmation & Gratitude

"I am grateful for the abundance in my life, and I attract even more blessings with an open heart."

Libra
18-March-2025

Today, dear Libra, a spiritual journey may call to you. Take time to meditate, reflect, or connect with your higher self. Spiritual practices will help you gain clarity and wisdom as you navigate life's path.

Affirmation & Gratitude

"I connect with my higher self, embracing the wisdom and peace that come from within."

Libra
19-March-2025

Today, dear Libra, expect the unexpected. Life may throw a curveball, but trust that it's guiding you toward growth and opportunity. Stay flexible and open-minded, and you'll find hidden blessings in the surprises that come your way.

Affirmation & Gratitude

"I welcome the unexpected, trusting that the universe is guiding me toward greater possibilities."

Libra

20-March-2025

Today, dear Libra, relationships are in focus. Whether it's with family, friends, or a partner, take time to strengthen your connections. Meaningful conversations and acts of kindness will deepen bonds and create lasting harmony.

Affirmation & Gratitude

"I nurture my relationships with love and care, building deeper connections with those I cherish."

Libra
21-March-2025

Today, dear Libra, it's time to focus on your goals. Use this day to reassess your plans and make any necessary adjustments. Stay determined and trust that your hard work is paving the way for success.

Affirmation & Gratitude

"I stay focused on my goals, trusting that each step brings me closer to success."

Libra

22-March-2025

Today, dear Libra, creativity flows effortlessly. Channel your artistic energy into something that excites you, whether it's a personal project or an innovative solution to a problem. Let your imagination lead the way.

Affirmation & Gratitude

"I celebrate the power of my creativity and let my imagination flow freely."

Libra
23-March-2025

Today, dear Libra, focus on health and wellbeing. Pay attention to your physical body and make choices that support your vitality. Whether it's exercise, healthy eating, or rest, small acts of care will bring long-lasting benefits.

Affirmation & Gratitude

"I nurture my body with love and care, honoring the temple that supports me."

Libra
24-March-2025

Today, dear Libra, communication is key. Whether it's a difficult conversation or simply expressing your thoughts, approach your interactions with honesty and clarity. Your ability to diplomatically handle situations will create harmony and understanding.

Affirmation & Gratitude

"I communicate clearly and honestly, fostering understanding in all my relationships."

Libra

25-March-2025

Today, dear Libra, focus on financial matters. Take time to evaluate your budget or investments, and make smart decisions for the future. Thoughtful planning today will lead to long-term security and abundance.

Affirmation & Gratitude

"I make wise financial choices that support my long-term stability and prosperity."

Libra
26-March-2025

Today, dear Libra, a sense of peace washes over you. Embrace the calm energy and take time to relax and recharge. You've been working hard, and now it's time to enjoy a moment of rest and reflection.

Affirmation & Gratitude

"I embrace peace and stillness, allowing myself to rest and recharge with ease."

Libra
27-March-2025

Today, dear Libra, personal growth is in focus. Consider where you want to improve and take actionable steps toward self-development. Even small efforts will lead to meaningful changes in the long run.

Affirmation & Gratitude

"I embrace personal growth, knowing that each small step brings me closer to becoming my best self."

Libra

28-March-2025

Today, dear Libra, love and relationships take center stage. Spend quality time with those you care about, and let your heart guide your interactions. Acts of kindness and compassion will strengthen the bonds you share with others.

Affirmation & Gratitude

"I nurture my relationships with love and care, building deeper connections with those I cherish."

Libra
29-March-2025

Today, dear Libra, focus on your passions. Whether it's a hobby, career, or personal project, channel your energy into what excites you. Following your passions will bring joy and fulfillment into your life.

Affirmation & Gratitude

"I follow my passions, knowing that they bring joy and purpose to my life."

Libra

30-March-2025

Today, dear Libra, it's time to let go of what no longer serves you. Whether it's a habit, a relationship, or a mindset, release it with love and gratitude. By letting go, you create space for new and better things to enter your life.

Affirmation & Gratitude

"I release what no longer serves me, making room for growth and new possibilities."

Libra

31-March-2025

Today, dear Libra, focus on gratitude. Reflect on the blessings in your life and express appreciation for all you've accomplished. Gratitude will open the door to even more abundance and joy in your world.

Affirmation & Gratitude

"I am grateful for all the blessings in my life, and I welcome even more abundance with an open heart."

April 2025

Libra
01-April-2025

Today, dear Libra, let your playful side out. Embrace lighthearted fun and enjoy the joy of the present moment. Humor and laughter will uplift your spirit and those around you. Take time to unwind and be carefree today.

Affirmation & Gratitude

"I embrace the joy and playfulness of life, filling my day with laughter and light."

Libra
02-April-2025

Today, dear Libra, focus on your personal goals. Set clear intentions for the coming weeks, and take small, actionable steps to achieve them. Your determination will lead to success, but remember to stay patient and trust the process.

Affirmation & Gratitude

"I set clear intentions and trust that my efforts will lead to success."

Libra

03-April-2025

Today, dear Libra, relationships require your attention. Whether it's a friend, partner, or family member, focus on building deeper connections. Honest communication and acts of kindness will strengthen your bonds and bring greater harmony into your life.

Affirmation & Gratitude

"I nurture my relationships with love, trust, and open communication."

Libra

04-April-2025

Today, dear Libra, your leadership qualities shine. Take charge of a project or guide others with confidence and compassion. Your ability to inspire and lead with fairness will bring success to both personal and professional endeavors.

Affirmation & Gratitude

"I lead with confidence and compassion, creating harmony and success in my path."

Libra
05-April-2025

Today, dear Libra, focus on creativity. Whether it's through art, writing, or problem-solving, let your imagination guide you. Don't be afraid to think outside the box and express yourself in unique ways.

Affirmation & Gratitude

"I embrace my creative spirit and let my imagination flow freely."

Libra

06-April-2025

Today, dear Libra, you may face a decision that requires careful consideration. Weigh your options thoughtfully and trust your intuition to guide you. Clarity will come when you listen to your inner voice and act with confidence.

Affirmation & Gratitude

"I trust my intuition and make decisions with clarity and confidence."

Libra
07-April-2025

Today, dear Libra, balance is key. You may feel pulled in different directions, but it's essential to prioritize self-care and set boundaries. Maintaining inner harmony will help you navigate the day with grace.

Affirmation & Gratitude

"I create balance in my life by honoring my needs and setting healthy boundaries."

Libra
08-April-2025

Today, dear Libra, financial matters may require attention. Review your budget, investments, or long-term plans. Thoughtful choices made today will lead to future security and peace of mind.

Affirmation & Gratitude

"I make wise financial decisions that support my long-term stability and prosperity."

Libra
09-April-2025

Today, dear Libra, focus on your personal growth. It's a great day to dive into self-reflection and set goals for improvement. Every step, no matter how small, contributes to your journey of becoming the best version of yourself.

Affirmation & Gratitude

"I embrace personal growth, knowing that each step brings me closer to my true potential."

Libra
10-April-2025

Today, dear Libra, your social charm shines. It's a great day for connecting with others and building new relationships. Your positive energy will attract meaningful connections and help you network in both personal and professional settings.

Affirmation & Gratitude

"I radiate positivity and attract meaningful connections into my life."

Libra
11-April-2025

Today, dear Libra, focus on emotional healing. If there are unresolved feelings or past wounds, now is the time to address them. Allow yourself to release what no longer serves you and make space for inner peace.

Affirmation & Gratitude

"I release emotional baggage and welcome healing and peace into my life."

Libra
12-April-2025

Today, dear Libra, a surge of creativity fills the air. Whether it's a personal project, a new hobby, or problem-solving, trust your innovative ideas. Your imagination is powerful today, so don't hesitate to explore fresh, out-of-the-box concepts.

Affirmation & Gratitude

"I celebrate my creativity and let my imagination guide me to new possibilities."

Libra
13-April-2025

Today, dear Libra, expect a wave of nostalgia. Reconnecting with your past or revisiting old memories can bring clarity and healing. Reflect on your journey and acknowledge how far you've come, but stay grounded in the present.

Affirmation & Gratitude

"I honor my past while embracing the beauty and opportunities of the present moment."

Libra
14-April-2025

Today, dear Libra, balance between work and play is essential. You may feel pressure to meet deadlines, but it's equally important to take time to unwind. Prioritize your mental health by balancing productivity with relaxation.

Affirmation & Gratitude

"I find harmony in balancing work and rest, ensuring my mind and body are cared for."

Libra
15-April-2025

Today, dear Libra, a significant opportunity may present itself. Trust your instincts and take a leap of faith if it feels right. Whether it's a career move or a personal decision, this chance has the potential to bring growth and fulfillment.

Affirmation & Gratitude

"I trust my instincts and embrace opportunities that lead to my growth and success."

Libra
16-April-2025

Today, dear Libra, focus on communication. Whether in personal or professional settings, clear and honest conversations will help resolve misunderstandings and build stronger relationships. Your words have power today, so use them wisely.

Affirmation & Gratitude

"I communicate clearly and with intention, creating harmony in all my relationships."

Libra
17-April-2025

Today, dear Libra, focus on self-love. Take time to nurture yourself and engage in activities that bring you joy and relaxation. Pampering your mind, body, and spirit will replenish your energy and boost your overall wellbeing.

Affirmation & Gratitude

"I prioritize self-care and nourish my mind, body, and soul with love and kindness."

Libra
18-April-2025

Today, dear Libra, new possibilities arise. Stay open to opportunities that may come from unexpected places. A flexible mindset will help you adapt and seize the moments that lead to growth and success.

Affirmation & Gratitude

"I embrace new opportunities with an open mind, trusting that the universe is guiding me."

Libra

19-April-2025

Today, dear Libra, focus on your health and wellness. Whether it's through physical activity, mindfulness, or nourishing your body with healthy foods, make your wellbeing a priority. Small steps today will lead to lasting benefits.

Affirmation & Gratitude

"I honor my body and mind by nurturing them with care and attention."

Libra

20-April-2025

Today, dear Libra, it's time to let go of what no longer serves you. Whether it's old habits, beliefs, or emotional baggage, release it with love and make space for new growth and experiences.

Affirmation & Gratitude

"I release what no longer serves me, creating space for growth and new possibilities."

Libra
21-April-2025

Today, dear Libra, focus on teamwork. Collaboration and mutual support will lead to success in your projects. Trust the power of working together and appreciate the unique talents of those around you.

Affirmation & Gratitude

"I embrace the strength of teamwork, knowing that together we achieve greater things."

Libra

22-April-2025

Today, dear Libra, gratitude is your key to happiness. Take time to reflect on the blessings in your life and express appreciation. Gratitude will attract even more abundance and positivity into your world.

Affirmation & Gratitude

"I am grateful for the blessings in my life, and I attract more joy and abundance every day."

Libra

23-April-2025

Today, dear Libra, focus on organization. Clearing physical or mental clutter will bring clarity and a sense of accomplishment. Take the time to tidy your space or reassess your priorities, and you'll feel more at peace.

Affirmation & Gratitude

"I create order in my life, clearing space for peace and productivity."

Libra
24-April-2025

Today, dear Libra, adventure calls. Whether it's a new experience, hobby, or travel, embrace the unknown with excitement. Stepping outside your comfort zone will bring fresh insights and joy into your life.

Affirmation & Gratitude

"I welcome adventure into my life, knowing that new experiences bring growth and joy."

Libra

25-April-2025

Today, dear Libra, a wave of inspiration comes your way. Use this creative energy to brainstorm new ideas or start a new project. Trust that your innovative thinking will lead to exciting opportunities.

Affirmation & Gratitude

"I welcome inspiration and creativity into my life, knowing they open doors to new possibilities."

Libra
26-April-2025

Today, dear Libra, focus on emotional healing. A heart-to-heart conversation or journaling your thoughts can bring clarity and release. Allow yourself to process your emotions with compassion and let go of what's been holding you back.

Affirmation & Gratitude

"I heal my emotions with compassion, releasing what no longer serves me."

Libra
27-April-2025

Today, dear Libra, relationships are highlighted. Nurture your close connections by being present and listening with an open heart. Small acts of kindness and understanding will deepen the bonds you share with loved ones.

Affirmation & Gratitude

"I nurture my relationships with love and compassion, strengthening the bonds I hold dear."

Libra

28-April-2025

Today, dear Libra, focus on setting goals for the future. It's a great day to plan ahead and create a clear vision for where you want to go. Trust that the universe will support your aspirations.

Affirmation & Gratitude

"I set clear goals for my future, knowing that the universe aligns to support my dreams."

Libra
29-April-2025

Today, dear Libra, a breakthrough moment may occur. Whether in work or personal life, something you've been waiting for will finally come to fruition. Stay open and ready to receive the rewards of your patience and hard work.

Affirmation & Gratitude

"I am open to receiving the breakthroughs and blessings that are coming my way."

Libra
30-April-2025

Today, dear Libra, peace and relaxation are calling. Take time to rest, meditate, or simply enjoy quiet moments of solitude. Recharging your energy will help you start the next month feeling refreshed and focused.

Affirmation & Gratitude

"I embrace peace and stillness, allowing myself to rest and recharge with ease."

May 2025

Libra
01-May-2025

Today, dear Libra, your focus is on renewal. A fresh start is on the horizon, so let go of the old and embrace the new. This is a time to set intentions for the month ahead, manifesting what you desire.

Affirmation & Gratitude

"I welcome new beginnings with an open heart, allowing positive change to flow into my life."

Libra
02-May-2025

Today, dear Libra, balance is key. You may feel torn between responsibilities, but by organizing your time and prioritizing self-care, you will maintain harmony. Don't forget to recharge when needed.

Affirmation & Gratitude

"I find balance by prioritizing my wellbeing, creating harmony in all areas of my life."

Libra
03-May-2025

Today, dear Libra, communication is highlighted. It's a great day to clear the air and express your thoughts openly. Whether in personal or professional settings, honest conversations will strengthen your connections and resolve any misunderstandings.

Affirmation & Gratitude

"I communicate openly and with kindness, fostering understanding in all my relationships."

Libra
04-May-2025

Today, dear Libra, your social side shines. Reconnect with old friends or meet new people. Laughter and shared moments will fill your day with joy, bringing warmth to your heart. Surround yourself with positive energy.

Affirmation & Gratitude

"I enjoy the beauty of meaningful connections, creating joyful moments with those I care about."

Libra

05-May-2025

Today, dear Libra, focus on long-term goals. Reevaluate where you want to be, and make adjustments to your plans. Patience and perseverance are essential now, as your efforts will pay off in the future.

Affirmation & Gratitude

"I stay focused on my long-term vision, trusting that every step brings me closer to success."

Libra
06-May-2025

Today, dear Libra, a surge of creativity flows through you. Embrace your artistic side or find innovative solutions to problems. This is a great day for brainstorming and bringing fresh ideas to life. Let your imagination lead the way.

Affirmation & Gratitude

"I embrace my creative energy and trust in the power of my imagination to create new possibilities."

Libra

07-May-2025

Today, dear Libra, a sense of calm surrounds you. Take time to relax, meditate, or engage in activities that bring peace. Recharging your mental and emotional energy will help you stay grounded and focused.

Affirmation & Gratitude

"I find peace in stillness and allow myself to recharge, knowing it supports my overall wellbeing."

Libra

08-May-2025

Today, dear Libra, it's time to take action. Whether in career, relationships, or personal goals, this is the moment to move forward confidently. The universe supports your steps toward growth and success.

Affirmation & Gratitude

"I take confident action, trusting that the universe is guiding me toward my highest potential."

Libra

09-May-2025

Today, dear Libra, relationships are at the forefront. Show appreciation for your loved ones through small gestures of kindness. Connection and harmony are essential today, so be present and open-hearted in your interactions.

Affirmation & Gratitude

"I nurture my relationships with love and care, creating deeper bonds with those I cherish."

Libra
10-May-2025

Today, dear Libra, focus on your physical wellbeing. Make healthy choices that support your vitality, whether through exercise, nutrition, or relaxation. Small changes today will have a big impact on your overall health.

Affirmation & Gratitude

"I honor my body by making healthy choices that support my energy and wellbeing."

Libra
11-May-2025

Today, dear Libra, financial matters may require attention. Reassess your budget or investments, and make thoughtful decisions that support your long-term goals. Practicality and foresight will ensure future abundance.

Affirmation & Gratitude

"I make wise financial choices that lead to security and prosperity."

Libra

12-May-2025

Today, dear Libra, a wave of optimism surrounds you. Believe in your ability to manifest positive outcomes, and trust that good things are coming your way. Your mindset will shape your reality, so keep your thoughts aligned with your desires.

Affirmation & Gratitude

"I attract positivity and abundance by believing in the power of my thoughts and intentions."

Libra
13-May-2025

Today, dear Libra, focus on personal growth. Whether it's through learning a new skill or deepening your self-awareness, take steps toward becoming the best version of yourself. Growth comes through consistent effort and reflection.

Affirmation & Gratitude

"I embrace opportunities for personal growth, knowing that each step leads to my highest potential."

Libra

14-May-2025

Today, dear Libra, emotions may surface. Allow yourself to feel deeply and process your feelings with compassion. Vulnerability leads to healing, so don't shy away from expressing your true emotions.

Affirmation & Gratitude

"I embrace my emotions with kindness, allowing them to guide me toward healing and understanding."

Libra
15-May-2025

Today, dear Libra, creativity is your guiding force. Dive into artistic pursuits or think outside the box to solve problems. Your unique ideas have the potential to bring excitement and innovation into your world.

Affirmation & Gratitude

"I celebrate my creativity and allow my imagination to flow freely, bringing fresh ideas to life."

Libra
16-May-2025

Today, dear Libra, focus on harmony. Whether in personal relationships or work environments, your ability to create peace and balance will be invaluable today. Your calming influence will help resolve conflicts and bring people together.

Affirmation & Gratitude

"I create harmony wherever I go, fostering peace and understanding in all my interactions."

Libra
17-May-2025

Today, dear Libra, adventure awaits. Step outside your comfort zone and embrace new experiences, whether it's a trip, a hobby, or meeting new people. Embrace the excitement of exploration and the growth it brings.

Affirmation & Gratitude

"I welcome new adventures and experiences, trusting that they will bring joy and growth into my life."

Libra
18-May-2025

Today, dear Libra, take time for self-reflection. Meditation or journaling will help you gain clarity on your inner thoughts and emotions. Trust the wisdom that comes from within, and use it to guide your next steps.

Affirmation & Gratitude

"I trust my inner wisdom, allowing it to guide me toward clarity and peace."

Libra
19-May-2025

Today, dear Libra, focus on teamwork. Collaborating with others will lead to success, whether in work or personal projects. Appreciate the strengths of those around you, and trust that working together will create something greater than the sum of its parts.

Affirmation & Gratitude

"I embrace the power of collaboration, knowing that teamwork brings greater success and fulfillment."

Libra

20-May-2025

Today, dear Libra, balance is key. You may feel pulled in multiple directions, but staying grounded and prioritizing your wellbeing will help you manage everything smoothly. Don't be afraid to set boundaries where needed.

Affirmation & Gratitude

"I maintain balance by honoring my needs and setting healthy boundaries in all areas of my life."

Libra

21-May-2025

Today, dear Libra, focus on gratitude. Take time to appreciate the beauty in your life, from small moments of joy to the larger blessings you've received. Expressing gratitude will attract even more abundance into your world.

Affirmation & Gratitude

"I am grateful for the blessings in my life, and I welcome even more joy and abundance with an open heart."

Libra

22-May-2025

Today, dear Libra, focus on communication. Your ability to express yourself clearly will strengthen your relationships and resolve any lingering misunderstandings. Be mindful of your words, and listen as much as you speak.

Affirmation & Gratitude

"I communicate with clarity and kindness, fostering understanding and harmony in all my relationships."

Libra

23-May-2025

Today, dear Libra, focus on personal goals. Set intentions for what you want to achieve in the coming weeks, and create a plan of action. Consistent effort will lead to success, so stay committed to your vision.

Affirmation & Gratitude

"I set clear goals and take consistent steps toward achieving them, trusting in my ability to succeed."

Libra

24-May-2025

Today, dear Libra, your social charm shines. It's a great day to connect with friends or network professionally. Your positive energy will attract meaningful connections, and new opportunities may arise from the conversations you have today.

Affirmation & Gratitude

"I radiate positivity and attract meaningful connections into my life, opening doors to new opportunities."

Libra

25-May-2025

Today, dear Libra, focus on rest and relaxation. You've been working hard, and now it's time to recharge. Whether through meditation, nature, or simply taking time off, nurturing yourself today will restore your energy and clarity.

Affirmation & Gratitude

"I give myself permission to rest and recharge, knowing that it supports my overall wellbeing."

Libra

26-May-2025

Today, dear Libra, creativity and innovation are your strongest allies. Let your imagination run wild, and don't hesitate to approach challenges with fresh, out-of-the-box solutions. Your unique ideas will lead to breakthroughs.

Affirmation & Gratitude

"I embrace my creative energy, allowing it to guide me toward innovative solutions and exciting opportunities."

Libra
27-May-2025

Today, dear Libra, focus on financial security. Take time to review your budget or investments and make adjustments that align with your long-term goals. Thoughtful planning today will ensure future abundance and peace of mind.

Affirmation & Gratitude

"I make wise financial choices that lead to security and prosperity in the long run."

Libra

28-May-2025

Today, dear Libra, relationships are highlighted. Whether romantic or platonic, nurturing your connections through meaningful conversations and acts of love will deepen your bonds. Be present and attentive with those who matter most.

Affirmation & Gratitude

"I nurture my relationships with love and care, building deeper connections with those I cherish."

Libra

29-May-2025

Today, dear Libra, expect the unexpected. Stay flexible and open to change, as new opportunities may arise from surprising places. Embrace the twists and turns with grace, trusting that they lead to growth and expansion.

Affirmation & Gratitude

"I welcome the unexpected, knowing that change brings new opportunities for growth and success."

Libra
30-May-2025

Today, dear Libra, focus on self-care. Take time to pamper yourself and prioritize your physical, mental, and emotional wellbeing. Small acts of kindness toward yourself will go a long way in restoring your energy and happiness.

Affirmation & Gratitude

"I honor myself by prioritizing self-care, knowing that I deserve love, kindness, and rest."

Libra

31-May-2025

Today, dear Libra, focus on spiritual growth. Engage in meditation, reflection, or any practice that connects you to your inner wisdom. Spiritual insights gained today will help you navigate life with greater peace and clarity.

Affirmation & Gratitude

"I connect with my inner self, embracing the wisdom and peace that come from spiritual growth."

June 2025

Libra
01-June-2025

Today, dear Libra, focus on fresh beginnings. A new chapter is unfolding, and it's the perfect time to set intentions for the month. Be open to new experiences and opportunities that align with your growth.

Affirmation & Gratitude

"I welcome fresh beginnings and new opportunities, trusting that they bring positive change into my life."

Libra
02-June-2025

Today, dear Libra, balance is key. You may feel stretched in multiple directions, but with organization and self-care, you can maintain harmony. Prioritize tasks wisely, and don't be afraid to delegate where needed.

Affirmation & Gratitude

"I maintain balance by prioritizing my time and energy, creating harmony in all areas of my life."

Libra
03-June-2025

Today, dear Libra, communication is your strength. Use your diplomatic nature to resolve any tensions or misunderstandings. Clear and compassionate dialogue will deepen connections and bring peace to your relationships.

Affirmation & Gratitude

"I communicate with clarity and kindness, fostering understanding and harmony in all my relationships."

Libra
04-June-2025

Today, dear Libra, focus on your creative energy. Whether it's an artistic pursuit or finding innovative solutions to challenges, let your imagination flow. Your unique perspective will lead to exciting opportunities.

Affirmation & Gratitude

"I embrace my creativity and allow my imagination to guide me toward new possibilities."

Libra
05-June-2025

Today, dear Libra, your social nature shines. It's a great day to connect with friends or network professionally. Meaningful conversations and joyful moments with loved ones will lift your spirit and open doors to new opportunities.

Affirmation & Gratitude

"I cherish my connections with others, creating joy and opportunity through meaningful interactions."

Libra

06-June-2025

Today, dear Libra, focus on personal goals. Reassess your long-term plans and make necessary adjustments. Stay patient and trust that your efforts will lead to success. Consistency is key, so stay committed to your vision.

Affirmation & Gratitude

"I stay focused on my long-term goals, knowing that every step brings me closer to success."

Libra
07-June-2025

Today, dear Libra, expect the unexpected. Surprising opportunities may arise, so remain open to new possibilities. Flexibility and adaptability will help you navigate these changes with grace, turning them into positive experiences.

Affirmation & Gratitude

"I embrace change with flexibility, trusting that it brings new opportunities for growth and expansion."

Libra
08-June-2025

Today, dear Libra, emotions may run high. Take time to process your feelings and approach any conflicts with calm and understanding. Vulnerability is a strength, so don't hesitate to share your emotions with those you trust.

Affirmation & Gratitude

"I embrace my emotions with compassion, allowing them to guide me toward healing and connection."

Libra
09-June-2025

Today, dear Libra, focus on harmony in your relationships. Whether at home or at work, your ability to create balance and peace will help resolve any tensions. Act as a mediator if needed, and your calm demeanor will inspire others.

Affirmation & Gratitude

"I bring peace and balance to my relationships, fostering harmony in all my interactions."

Libra
10-June-2025

Today, dear Libra, it's time for action. Whether in your career or personal life, take confident steps forward toward your goals. Trust that the universe is supporting you as you move closer to achieving your dreams.

Affirmation & Gratitude

"I take bold and confident steps toward my goals, trusting that the universe supports my journey."

Libra
11-June-2025

Today, dear Libra, focus on self-care. You've been giving a lot of your energy lately, and now it's time to recharge. Whether through relaxation, exercise, or meditation, taking care of your physical and mental health is essential today.

Affirmation & Gratitude

"I honor my body and mind by nurturing them with love, rest, and care."

Libra

12-June-2025

Today, dear Libra, collaboration is key. Working together with others will lead to success, whether in personal projects or professional endeavors. Appreciate the unique strengths of those around you, and trust that teamwork will create something greater.

Affirmation & Gratitude

"I embrace collaboration, knowing that teamwork leads to greater success and fulfillment."

Libra
13-June-2025

Today, dear Libra, focus on gratitude. Take time to appreciate the blessings in your life, no matter how small. Expressing gratitude will attract even more abundance into your world, filling your heart with joy and contentment.

Affirmation & Gratitude

"I am grateful for the blessings in my life, and I attract even more abundance through my gratitude."

Libra
14-June-2025

Today, dear Libra, new opportunities may arise. Stay open to possibilities, even if they seem outside your comfort zone. Trust that stepping into the unknown will lead to growth and exciting developments in both personal and professional areas.

Affirmation & Gratitude

"I welcome new opportunities with an open heart, trusting that they lead to growth and success."

Libra
15-June-2025

Today, dear Libra, focus on relationships. Nurture the bonds with your loved ones by spending quality time together. Meaningful conversations and acts of kindness will deepen your connections and bring joy to your day.

Affirmation & Gratitude

"I nurture my relationships with love and care, creating deeper connections with those I cherish."

Libra
16-June-2025

Today, dear Libra, financial matters may require attention. Take time to review your budget, savings, or investments, and make thoughtful decisions that align with your long-term goals. Practicality and planning today will bring future abundance.

Affirmation & Gratitude

"I make wise financial choices that support my long-term stability and prosperity."

Libra
17-June-2025

Today, dear Libra, creativity flows effortlessly. Use this energy to dive into a new project or explore innovative solutions to challenges. Your artistic and imaginative side will help you find unique ways to express yourself and solve problems.

Affirmation & Gratitude

"I celebrate my creativity and trust in my ability to bring fresh, innovative ideas to life."

Libra
18-June-2025

Today, dear Libra, focus on your physical health. Whether through exercise, healthy eating, or simply taking time to relax, pay attention to your body's needs. Small acts of care today will lead to long-term wellbeing and vitality.

Affirmation & Gratitude

"I honor my body by nurturing it with love and care, creating long-lasting health and vitality."

Libra
19-June-2025

Today, dear Libra, balance is your mantra. You may feel pulled in multiple directions, but with thoughtful planning and self-care, you'll maintain harmony. Remember to set boundaries where needed and prioritize what's most important.

Affirmation & Gratitude

"I maintain balance by setting boundaries and prioritizing what truly matters to me."

Libra

20-June-2025

Today, dear Libra, it's time to take action. Whether in career, relationships, or personal goals, move forward with confidence and determination. The universe supports your steps toward growth and success, so trust your instincts.

Affirmation & Gratitude

"I take decisive action, trusting that each step brings me closer to achieving my dreams."

Libra
21-June-2025

Today, dear Libra, focus on self-reflection. Journaling, meditation, or quiet time in nature will help you connect with your inner thoughts and emotions. By tuning in to your inner self, you'll gain clarity on your next steps.

Affirmation & Gratitude

"I connect with my inner wisdom, trusting that it guides me toward clarity and peace."

Libra

22-June-2025

Today, dear Libra, adventure calls! Step out of your routine and embrace new experiences. Whether it's trying a new activity or exploring new places, allowing yourself to be spontaneous will bring excitement and joy into your day.

Affirmation & Gratitude

"I welcome adventure into my life, knowing that new experiences bring growth and joy."

Libra
23-June-2025

Today, dear Libra, focus on building harmony in your relationships. Clear communication and acts of kindness will strengthen your bonds and create peace in your interactions. Today is a day for unity and understanding.

Affirmation & Gratitude

"I create harmony in my relationships by communicating with love and understanding."

Libra
24-June-2025

Today, dear Libra, focus on long-term goals. It's a great day to plan ahead, setting intentions for the months to come. Take small, consistent steps toward your vision, and trust that the universe will support your efforts.

Affirmation & Gratitude

"I set clear goals and take steady steps toward achieving my dreams, trusting that the universe supports me."

Libra
25-June-2025

Today, dear Libra, your social charm is at its peak. Reach out to friends, colleagues, or loved ones and enjoy meaningful conversations. Your positive energy will attract good vibes and help build stronger connections.

Affirmation & Gratitude

"I radiate positivity and joy, creating deeper connections with those around me."

Libra
26-June-2025

Today, dear Libra, it's time to focus on personal growth. Whether it's learning something new or deepening your self-awareness, take steps toward becoming the best version of yourself. Growth comes from consistent effort and reflection.

Affirmation & Gratitude

"I embrace opportunities for personal growth, knowing that each step leads me to my highest potential."

Libra
27-June-2025

Today, dear Libra, take time for self-care. You've been working hard, and now it's important to recharge. Whether through relaxation, pampering, or simply taking a break, nurturing yourself today will restore your energy and clarity.

Affirmation & Gratitude

"I honor myself by taking time to rest and recharge, knowing that I deserve love and care."

Libra
28-June-2025

Today, dear Libra, financial matters may require attention. Take time to reassess your budget or investments, making adjustments that support your long-term security. Thoughtful planning today will ensure future abundance.

Affirmation & Gratitude

"I make wise financial decisions that lead to long-term security and prosperity."

Libra

29-June-2025

Today, dear Libra, focus on creativity. Whether it's a personal project, an artistic endeavor, or simply finding innovative solutions to challenges, let your imagination lead the way. Your unique perspective will open doors to exciting possibilities.

Affirmation & Gratitude

"I trust my creative energy to guide me toward new ideas and exciting opportunities."

Libra

30-June-2025

Today, dear Libra, reflection and rest are needed. Take time to unwind and recharge after a busy month. By slowing down and practicing mindfulness, you'll gain clarity and set the stage for the coming days.

Affirmation & Gratitude

"I give myself permission to rest and reflect, knowing that it brings clarity and peace."

July 2025

Libra
01-July-2025

Today, dear Libra, fresh energy fills the air. Set your intentions for the month ahead, and focus on manifesting your desires. Trust that the universe supports your aspirations and is guiding you toward success.

Affirmation & Gratitude

"I set clear intentions and trust that the universe is aligning to support my dreams."

Libra
02-July-2025

Today, dear Libra, balance is key. With various responsibilities pulling at you, remember to prioritize both work and rest. Maintaining inner harmony will keep you centered as you navigate through the day's demands.

Affirmation & Gratitude

"I create balance in my life by honoring both my responsibilities and my need for rest."

Libra
03-July-2025

Today, dear Libra, communication is essential. Be clear and open in your interactions, especially if tensions arise. Your diplomatic nature will help resolve conflicts and bring harmony to any situation.

Affirmation & Gratitude

"I communicate with honesty and kindness, fostering understanding and peace in my relationships."

Libra
04-July-2025

Today, dear Libra, focus on creativity. Let your imagination guide you, whether in artistic pursuits or problem-solving. Fresh ideas will flow easily today, so embrace your inventive side and explore new possibilities.

Affirmation & Gratitude

"I embrace my creativity and trust in my ability to bring fresh ideas to life."

Libra

05-July-2025

Today, dear Libra, relationships take center stage. Show your loved ones how much you care with small gestures of kindness and thoughtful conversations. Strengthen your bonds by being present and attentive.

Affirmation & Gratitude

"I nurture my relationships with love and attention, building deeper connections with those I cherish."

Libra

06-July-2025

Today, dear Libra, focus on personal growth. Take time to reflect on where you are and where you want to be. Self-awareness and a commitment to growth will lead you closer to becoming the best version of yourself.

Affirmation & Gratitude

"I embrace personal growth, knowing that every step brings me closer to my highest potential."

Libra
07-July-2025

Today, dear Libra, financial matters may require attention. Take a closer look at your budget, investments, or long-term financial plans. Practical decisions made today will secure your future prosperity and peace of mind.

Affirmation & Gratitude

"I make wise financial choices that support my long-term stability and success."

Libra

08-July-2025

Today, dear Libra, adventure calls! Step out of your routine and explore something new. Whether it's a new place, hobby, or experience, embracing the unknown will bring excitement and joy into your life.

Affirmation & Gratitude

"I welcome new adventures into my life, trusting that they bring joy and growth."

Libra
09-July-2025

Today, dear Libra, focus on collaboration. Working with others will lead to success, whether in personal projects or professional endeavors. Appreciate the strengths of those around you, and trust that teamwork will create something greater.

Affirmation & Gratitude

"I embrace the power of teamwork, knowing that collaboration brings greater success."

Libra
10-July-2025

Today, dear Libra, focus on self-care. You've been giving a lot of yourself lately, and now it's time to recharge. Whether through relaxation, mindfulness, or spending time in nature, nurturing yourself will restore your energy and clarity.

Affirmation & Gratitude

"I honor my body and mind by taking time to rest and recharge."

Libra
11-July-2025

Today, dear Libra, your social side shines. It's a great day to connect with friends, family, or colleagues. Your positive energy will attract meaningful connections and joyful moments, so embrace the opportunity to share laughter and lightheartedness.

Affirmation & Gratitude

"I radiate positivity and joy, creating meaningful connections with those around me."

Libra

12-July-2025

Today, dear Libra, new opportunities may arise. Stay open to possibilities, even if they seem unexpected or unconventional. Stepping out of your comfort zone will bring exciting growth and lead you toward success.

Affirmation & Gratitude

"I welcome new opportunities, trusting that they bring growth and positive change into my life."

Libra
13-July-2025

Today, dear Libra, emotions may surface. Take time to process your feelings and approach any conflicts with compassion and understanding. By embracing vulnerability, you'll foster deeper connections and healing in your relationships.

Affirmation & Gratitude

"I embrace my emotions with kindness, allowing them to guide me toward healing and connection."

Libra
14-July-2025

Today, dear Libra, focus on long-term goals. Reassess your plans and make adjustments as needed. Consistent effort and patience will bring the results you seek, so stay committed to your vision.

Affirmation & Gratitude

"I stay focused on my long-term goals, trusting that every step brings me closer to success."

Libra
15-July-2025

Today, dear Libra, creativity flows effortlessly. Use this energy to dive into a new project or explore fresh ideas. Whether artistic or practical, your innovative thinking will lead to exciting possibilities.

Affirmation & Gratitude

"I embrace my creative energy and allow my imagination to guide me toward new opportunities."

Libra
16-July-2025

Today, dear Libra, it's time for self-reflection. Journaling or quiet meditation will help you gain clarity on your inner thoughts and emotions. By connecting with yourself, you'll gain insight into your next steps.

Affirmation & Gratitude

"I connect with my inner wisdom, trusting that it guides me toward clarity and peace."

Libra
17-July-2025

Today, dear Libra, focus on gratitude. Take a moment to reflect on the blessings in your life and express appreciation for them. Gratitude will attract even more abundance and joy into your world.

Affirmation & Gratitude

"I am grateful for the blessings in my life, and I welcome even more abundance with an open heart."

Libra
18-July-2025

Today, dear Libra, expect the unexpected. Surprises may come your way, but stay flexible and embrace the changes with an open heart. These shifts will ultimately lead you toward growth and positive transformation.

Affirmation & Gratitude

"I welcome unexpected changes, trusting that they bring growth and new opportunities."

Libra
19-July-2025

Today, dear Libra, focus on relationships. Whether with friends, family, or a partner, spending quality time with loved ones will strengthen your bonds. Share joy, laughter, and meaningful conversations to deepen your connections.

Affirmation & Gratitude

"I nurture my relationships with love and care, creating deeper bonds with those I cherish."

Libra
20-July-2025

Today, dear Libra, financial planning is in focus. Take time to review your financial situation and make any necessary adjustments. Thoughtful decisions made today will lead to long-term security and abundance.

Affirmation & Gratitude

"I make wise financial choices that lead to stability and prosperity."

Libra
21-July-2025

Today, dear Libra, adventure awaits. Step out of your routine and try something new, whether it's a hobby, trip, or experience. Embracing the unknown will bring excitement and joy into your life.

Affirmation & Gratitude

"I embrace new adventures, trusting that they bring growth and joy into my life."

Libra

22-July-2025

Today, dear Libra, focus on your physical health. Pay attention to your body's needs, whether through exercise, healthy eating, or relaxation. Nurturing your physical wellbeing will enhance your overall vitality.

Affirmation & Gratitude

"I honor my body by nurturing it with love, care, and healthy choices."

Libra
23-July-2025

Today, dear Libra, creativity is your ally. Whether you're working on a personal project or solving a problem, trust your imaginative side. Your ability to think outside the box will lead to fresh solutions and exciting new ideas.

Affirmation & Gratitude

"I trust my creativity to guide me toward new ideas and exciting opportunities."

Libra

24-July-2025

Today, dear Libra, focus on teamwork. Collaboration will bring great success today, so lean on the strengths of those around you. Together, you can achieve something greater than you could alone.

Affirmation & Gratitude

"I embrace collaboration, knowing that teamwork leads to greater success and fulfillment."

Libra

25-July-2025

Today, dear Libra, communication is essential. Clear, honest conversations will strengthen your relationships and resolve any lingering misunderstandings. Speak your truth with kindness, and listen to others with an open heart.

Affirmation & Gratitude

"I communicate with clarity and kindness, fostering understanding in all my relationships."

Libra
26-July-2025

Today, dear Libra, focus on personal goals. Set clear intentions for the rest of the month and create a plan to achieve them. Consistent effort and focus will bring the results you seek, so stay determined.

Affirmation & Gratitude

"I set clear goals and take consistent steps toward achieving them, trusting in my ability to succeed."

Libra

27-July-2025

Today, dear Libra, emotions may run high. Take time to reflect on your feelings and approach conflicts with compassion. Vulnerability and openness will strengthen your relationships and bring healing where needed.

Affirmation & Gratitude

"I embrace my emotions with compassion, allowing them to guide me toward healing and understanding."

Libra
28-July-2025

Today, dear Libra, adventure beckons. Step outside your comfort zone and embrace new experiences, whether it's travel, a hobby, or meeting new people. New opportunities for growth and joy await.

Affirmation & Gratitude

"I welcome new adventures into my life, trusting that they bring joy and expansion."

Libra
29-July-2025

Today, dear Libra, focus on balance. With various demands on your time, it's essential to maintain inner harmony. Set boundaries where needed and make time for both work and relaxation.

Affirmation & Gratitude

"I maintain balance in my life by setting healthy boundaries and prioritizing self-care."

Libra
30-July-2025

Today, dear Libra, focus on self-care. You've been giving a lot of yourself lately, and now it's time to recharge. Whether through relaxation, mindfulness, or spending time in nature, nurturing yourself will restore your energy and peace.

Affirmation & Gratitude

"I nurture myself with love and care, allowing my body and mind to rest and recharge."

Libra
31-July-2025

Today, dear Libra, gratitude is the key to joy. Reflect on the blessings in your life and express appreciation for them. Gratitude will open the door to even more abundance and happiness in your world.

Affirmation & Gratitude

"I am grateful for the blessings in my life, and I welcome even more abundance with an open heart."

August 2025

Libra
01-August-2025

Today, dear Libra, focus on fresh beginnings. Set intentions for the new month and embrace the energy of change. A new opportunity may present itself, so stay open and adaptable. Trust that everything is unfolding as it should.

Affirmation & Gratitude

"I welcome new beginnings and embrace change, trusting that the universe is guiding me toward growth and success."

Libra
02-August-2025

Today, dear Libra, balance is essential. You may feel pulled in different directions, but maintaining inner harmony will help you manage everything smoothly. Prioritize your time and energy wisely, and don't hesitate to set boundaries where needed.

Affirmation & Gratitude

"I find balance by honoring my needs and setting healthy boundaries in all areas of my life."

Libra
03-August-2025

Today, dear Libra, focus on communication. Clear and honest conversations will resolve any misunderstandings and strengthen your relationships. Speak from the heart, and listen with empathy. Your ability to create harmony through words will shine today.

Affirmation & Gratitude

"I communicate with clarity and kindness, fostering understanding and harmony in all my relationships."

Libra
04-August-2025

Today, dear Libra, creativity flows effortlessly. Use this energy to dive into a new project or explore fresh ideas. Your imagination will guide you toward exciting possibilities, so don't hesitate to think outside the box and embrace innovation.

Affirmation & Gratitude

"I embrace my creative energy and trust in my ability to bring fresh, innovative ideas to life."

Libra

05-August-2025

Today, dear Libra, focus on relationships. Strengthen the bonds with your loved ones by being present and showing appreciation. Small acts of kindness and thoughtful gestures will deepen your connections and bring more joy into your day.

Affirmation & Gratitude

"I nurture my relationships with love and attention, building deeper connections with those I cherish."

Libra
06-August-2025

Today, dear Libra, take time for self-reflection. Journaling or quiet meditation will help you gain clarity on your inner thoughts and emotions. Trust your intuition, and allow yourself to explore what truly matters to you.

Affirmation & Gratitude

"I connect with my inner wisdom, trusting that it guides me toward clarity and peace."

Libra

07-August-2025

Today, dear Libra, financial planning is in focus. Take time to review your budget, savings, or investments, and make thoughtful decisions for the future. Practical steps taken today will ensure long-term stability and abundance.

Affirmation & Gratitude

"I make wise financial decisions that support my long-term security and prosperity."

Libra

08-August-2025

Today, dear Libra, adventure calls! Step out of your comfort zone and explore new experiences. Whether it's travel, a new hobby, or meeting new people, embracing the unknown will bring excitement and personal growth.

Affirmation & Gratitude

"I welcome new adventures into my life, trusting that they bring joy and expansion."

Libra

09-August-2025

Today, dear Libra, focus on self-care. You've been working hard, and now it's time to recharge. Whether through relaxation, pampering, or simply taking a break, nurturing yourself today will restore your energy and clarity.

Affirmation & Gratitude

"I honor myself by taking time to rest and recharge, knowing that I deserve love and care."

Libra
10-August-2025

Today, dear Libra, expect the unexpected. A surprise opportunity may arise, so stay flexible and open-minded. Change can lead to exciting new possibilities, so trust the process and embrace the journey ahead with confidence.

Affirmation & Gratitude

"I welcome unexpected changes, trusting that they bring growth and positive transformation into my life."

Libra
11-August-2025

Today, dear Libra, focus on collaboration. Working with others will lead to success, whether in personal projects or professional endeavors. Appreciate the unique strengths of those around you, and trust that teamwork will create something greater.

Affirmation & Gratitude

"I embrace the power of teamwork, knowing that collaboration brings greater success and fulfillment."

Libra
12-August-2025

Today, dear Libra, emotions may run high. Take time to process your feelings and approach any conflicts with compassion. Vulnerability will lead to healing, so don't hesitate to share your emotions with those you trust.

Affirmation & Gratitude

"I embrace my emotions with kindness, allowing them to guide me toward healing and deeper connections."

Libra
13-August-2025

Today, dear Libra, your social charm is highlighted. It's a great day to connect with friends, family, or colleagues. Meaningful conversations and shared moments of joy will strengthen your bonds and open doors to new opportunities.

Affirmation & Gratitude

"I radiate positivity and joy, creating meaningful connections with those around me."

Libra
14-August-2025

Today, dear Libra, focus on personal growth. Take steps toward becoming the best version of yourself by learning something new or deepening your self-awareness. Every small effort contributes to your journey of growth and transformation.

Affirmation & Gratitude

"I embrace opportunities for personal growth, knowing that each step brings me closer to my true potential."

Libra
15-August-2025

Today, dear Libra, financial matters may require attention. Review your budget or long-term plans, and make adjustments if needed. Thoughtful planning today will bring future security and abundance. Trust your instincts when making financial decisions.

Affirmation & Gratitude

"I make wise financial choices that lead to long-term security and prosperity."

Libra
16-August-2025

Today, dear Libra, creativity flows effortlessly. Use this energy to dive into a new project or explore fresh ideas. Whether it's artistic or practical, your innovative thinking will lead to exciting possibilities.

Affirmation & Gratitude

"I embrace my creative energy and trust in my ability to bring fresh ideas to life."

Libra
17-August-2025

Today, dear Libra, focus on self-care. You've been giving a lot of yourself lately, and now it's time to nurture your mind, body, and spirit. Pampering yourself with love and care will restore your energy and bring balance back into your life.

Affirmation & Gratitude

"I nurture myself with love and care, allowing my mind, body, and spirit to rest and recharge."

Libra
18-August-2025

Today, dear Libra, communication is key. Whether in personal or professional settings, clear and honest conversations will resolve misunderstandings and bring harmony. Use your diplomatic skills to create peace and understanding in all your interactions.

Affirmation & Gratitude

"I communicate with clarity and kindness, fostering understanding and harmony in all my relationships."

Libra

19-August-2025

Today, dear Libra, a wave of inspiration comes your way. Use this creative energy to brainstorm new ideas or start a new project. Trust that your innovative thinking will lead to exciting opportunities for growth and success.

Affirmation & Gratitude

"I welcome inspiration and creativity into my life, knowing they open doors to new possibilities."

Libra

20-August-2025

Today, dear Libra, relationships are in focus. Whether romantic or platonic, nurturing your connections through meaningful conversations and acts of love will deepen your bonds. Be present with those who matter most, and express your appreciation.

Affirmation & Gratitude

"I nurture my relationships with love and care, building deeper connections with those I cherish."

Libra

21-August-2025

Today, dear Libra, focus on long-term goals. It's a great day to reassess your plans and make adjustments if needed. Stay patient and committed to your vision, knowing that each step brings you closer to success.

Affirmation & Gratitude

"I stay focused on my long-term goals, trusting that every step brings me closer to success."

Libra

22-August-2025

Today, dear Libra, adventure awaits! Step out of your routine and embrace new experiences, whether through travel, a hobby, or meeting new people. Exploring the unknown will bring excitement and opportunities for growth.

Affirmation & Gratitude

"I embrace new adventures with an open heart, trusting that they bring joy and expansion."

Libra

23-August-2025

Today, dear Libra, focus on gratitude. Reflect on the blessings in your life, big or small, and express appreciation for them. Gratitude will attract even more abundance into your world and fill your heart with joy.

Affirmation & Gratitude

"I am grateful for the blessings in my life, and I welcome even more joy and abundance with an open heart."

Libra
24-August-2025

Today, dear Libra, emotions may run high. Take time to ground yourself and process your feelings before reacting. Approach any conflicts with calm and understanding, and let your emotions guide you toward healing and resolution.

Affirmation & Gratitude

"I embrace my emotions with kindness, allowing them to guide me toward healing and understanding."

Libra
25-August-2025

Today, dear Libra, collaboration is key. Working with others will lead to success, whether in personal or professional projects. Appreciate the unique talents of those around you, and trust that teamwork will bring greater results than working alone.

Affirmation & Gratitude

"I embrace collaboration, knowing that teamwork brings greater success and fulfillment."

Libra

26-August-2025

Today, dear Libra, focus on personal goals. Set clear intentions for what you want to achieve, and take actionable steps toward them. Consistency and dedication will bring the results you seek, so stay committed to your vision.

Affirmation & Gratitude

"I set clear goals and take consistent steps toward achieving them, trusting in my ability to succeed."

Libra
27-August-2025

Today, dear Libra, new opportunities may arise. Stay open to possibilities that may seem unexpected or unconventional. Taking a leap of faith could lead to exciting growth and success, so embrace change with confidence.

Affirmation & Gratitude

"I welcome new opportunities, trusting that they bring growth and positive transformation into my life."

Libra

28-August-2025

Today, dear Libra, focus on self-care. You've been giving a lot of yourself recently, and now it's time to rest and recharge. Prioritize your wellbeing and give yourself permission to slow down. Your mind, body, and spirit will thank you for it.

Affirmation & Gratitude

"I nurture my mind, body, and spirit by taking time to rest and recharge, knowing I deserve love and care."

Libra
29-August-2025

Today, dear Libra, creativity flows easily. Let your imagination run free and explore new projects or ideas. Whether through art, writing, or innovative problem-solving, your creative energy will guide you to exciting possibilities.

Affirmation & Gratitude

"I celebrate my creativity and trust my ability to bring fresh ideas and solutions to life."

Libra
30-August-2025

Today, dear Libra, focus on balance. You may feel pulled in different directions, but maintaining a sense of inner harmony will help you manage the day. Prioritize self-care, and remember that you don't have to do everything at once.

Affirmation & Gratitude

"I find balance by prioritizing my needs and setting boundaries, creating harmony in all areas of my life."

Libra

31-August-2025

Today, dear Libra, it's time to reflect on your journey. Take a moment to appreciate how far you've come and all you've accomplished. Celebrate your successes, big and small, and use this reflective energy to set new intentions for the month ahead.

Affirmation & Gratitude

"I honor my progress and celebrate the journey, trusting that I am always growing and evolving."

September 2025

Libra

01-September-2025

Today, dear Libra, new energy surrounds you. As the month begins, set your intentions and embrace the opportunities that await. Stay positive and focused on your goals, knowing that the universe is supporting you on your journey.

Affirmation & Gratitude

"I welcome the new month with positivity and set clear intentions for growth and success."

Libra

02-September-2025

Today, dear Libra, relationships take the spotlight. Nurture your connections by being present and attentive. Meaningful conversations and acts of kindness will strengthen your bonds and bring harmony into your interactions.

Affirmation & Gratitude

"I nurture my relationships with love and attention, creating deeper bonds with those I cherish."

Libra

03-September-2025

Today, dear Libra, creativity is abundant. Whether it's an artistic project or problem-solving, your imagination is your greatest asset today. Let your ideas flow freely, and trust that innovation will lead to exciting opportunities.

Affirmation & Gratitude

"I embrace my creativity and trust my ability to find new and exciting solutions."

Libra

04-September-2025

Today, dear Libra, focus on self-reflection. Quiet time alone will help you gain clarity on your thoughts and feelings. Meditate, journal, or simply sit in stillness to connect with your inner self and discover what truly matters to you.

Affirmation & Gratitude

"I connect with my inner self, allowing peace and clarity to guide my journey."

Libra

05-September-2025

Today, dear Libra, collaboration will bring success. Whether in work or personal projects, lean on the strengths of those around you. Working together as a team will create something greater than what you could achieve alone.

Affirmation & Gratitude

"I embrace the power of teamwork, knowing that collaboration brings greater success and fulfillment."

Libra

06-September-2025

Today, dear Libra, financial planning is key. Review your budget, savings, or long-term investments, and make thoughtful decisions to support your future stability. Practicality today will lead to prosperity tomorrow.

Affirmation & Gratitude

"I make wise financial choices that ensure my long-term security and abundance."

Libra

07-September-2025

Today, dear Libra, focus on adventure. Break free from your routine and try something new, whether it's a hobby, trip, or spontaneous activity. Embracing the unknown will bring joy and new experiences into your life.

Affirmation & Gratitude

"I welcome new adventures, knowing that they bring excitement and growth into my life."

Libra
08-September-2025

Today, dear Libra, communication is key. Clear, honest conversations will help resolve any lingering issues and strengthen your relationships. Speak your truth with kindness, and listen to others with an open heart.

Affirmation & Gratitude

"I communicate with clarity and kindness, fostering understanding and harmony in all my interactions."

Libra

09-September-2025

Today, dear Libra, focus on balance. With various responsibilities pulling at you, it's important to prioritize your time and energy wisely. Set boundaries where needed, and remember to take care of yourself as much as others.

Affirmation & Gratitude

"I create balance in my life by honoring my needs and setting healthy boundaries."

Libra
10-September-2025

Today, dear Libra, emotions may surface. Take time to process your feelings and approach any conflicts with compassion and understanding. Vulnerability leads to healing, so don't shy away from expressing your true emotions.

Affirmation & Gratitude

"I embrace my emotions with kindness, allowing them to guide me toward healing and deeper connections."

Libra

11-September-2025

Today, dear Libra, your social charm shines. It's a great day to connect with friends, family, or colleagues. Your positive energy will attract meaningful conversations and joyful moments, so embrace the opportunity to strengthen bonds with others.

Affirmation & Gratitude

"I radiate positivity and joy, creating meaningful connections with those around me."

Libra

12-September-2025

Today, dear Libra, focus on long-term goals. It's a great day to reassess your plans and make adjustments if needed. Stay patient and committed to your vision, knowing that each step brings you closer to success.

Affirmation & Gratitude

"I stay focused on my long-term goals, trusting that every step brings me closer to success."

Libra

13-September-2025

Today, dear Libra, adventure calls. Step outside your comfort zone and try something new. Whether it's a new place, hobby, or meeting new people, embracing the unknown will bring excitement and growth into your life.

Affirmation & Gratitude

"I welcome new experiences with an open heart, trusting that they bring joy and growth."

Libra

14-September-2025

Today, dear Libra, self-care is essential. You've been giving a lot of yourself lately, and now it's time to nurture your mind, body, and spirit. Rest, relax, and prioritize your wellbeing today, knowing that it will restore your energy.

Affirmation & Gratitude

"I honor myself by taking time to rest and recharge, knowing that I deserve love and care."

Libra

15-September-2025

Today, dear Libra, creativity flows effortlessly. Whether it's through art, writing, or finding innovative solutions, let your imagination guide you. Trust that your creative energy will lead you toward exciting new possibilities.

Affirmation & Gratitude

"I celebrate my creativity and trust in my ability to bring fresh ideas to life."

Libra

16-September-2025

Today, dear Libra, focus on relationships. Small acts of kindness and thoughtful gestures will go a long way in strengthening your connections. Show appreciation for those around you, and watch your relationships blossom with love and joy.

Affirmation & Gratitude

"I nurture my relationships with love and kindness, building deeper connections with those I care about."

Libra

17-September-2025

Today, dear Libra, financial matters may require attention. Take time to review your finances and make adjustments to your budget or investments if needed. Thoughtful planning today will ensure future security and peace of mind.

Affirmation & Gratitude

"I make wise financial choices that lead to security and prosperity."

Libra

18-September-2025

Today, dear Libra, emotions may be intense. Allow yourself to feel deeply, but stay grounded as you process your emotions. Meditation or quiet reflection will help you gain clarity and guide you toward healing.

Affirmation & Gratitude

"I embrace my emotions with compassion, allowing them to guide me toward healing and understanding."

Libra

19-September-2025

Today, dear Libra, focus on adventure. Break away from your routine and try something new, whether it's a spontaneous trip or a new activity. Embrace the unknown and allow yourself to explore the excitement of new experiences.

Affirmation & Gratitude

"I welcome new adventures, trusting that they bring growth and joy into my life."

Libra

20-September-2025

Today, dear Libra, focus on personal growth. Take steps toward becoming the best version of yourself by learning something new or deepening your self-awareness. Each small effort contributes to your journey of growth and transformation.

Affirmation & Gratitude

"I embrace opportunities for personal growth, knowing that each step brings me closer to my true potential."

Libra

21-September-2025

Today, dear Libra, financial planning is in focus. Review your long-term goals, savings, or investments, and make any necessary adjustments. Practical decisions made today will lead to future stability and abundance.

Affirmation & Gratitude

"I make wise financial decisions that support my long-term security and prosperity."

Libra

22-September-2025

Today, dear Libra, creativity is abundant. Whether you're starting a new project or solving a problem, trust your imaginative side. Your innovative ideas will bring fresh perspectives and lead you toward exciting new possibilities.

Affirmation & Gratitude

"I trust my creativity to guide me toward new and exciting opportunities."

Libra
23-September-2025

Today, dear Libra, relationships take center stage. Spend quality time with loved ones and strengthen your bonds through meaningful conversations. Acts of kindness and thoughtful gestures will deepen your connections and bring more joy into your day.

Affirmation & Gratitude

"I nurture my relationships with love and attention, building deeper connections with those I cherish."

Libra
24-September-2025

Today, dear Libra, focus on communication. Whether in personal or professional settings, clear and honest conversations will resolve any misunderstandings and strengthen your connections. Speak with kindness and listen with empathy.

Affirmation & Gratitude

"I communicate with clarity and kindness, fostering understanding and harmony in all my interactions."

Libra

25-September-2025

Today, dear Libra, emotions may run high. Take time to reflect on your feelings and approach any conflicts with compassion. Vulnerability and openness will strengthen your relationships and bring healing where needed.

Affirmation & Gratitude

"I embrace my emotions with compassion, allowing them to guide me toward healing and understanding."

Libra

26-September-2025

Today, dear Libra, focus on gratitude. Take a moment to appreciate the blessings in your life and express appreciation for them. Gratitude will attract even more abundance and joy into your world.

Affirmation & Gratitude

"I am grateful for the blessings in my life, and I welcome even more abundance with an open heart."

Libra

27-September-2025

Today, dear Libra, collaboration will lead to success. Working with others will bring new perspectives and greater results than working alone. Appreciate the strengths of those around you, and trust that teamwork will lead to exciting outcomes.

Affirmation & Gratitude

"I embrace the power of teamwork, knowing that collaboration brings greater success and fulfillment."

Libra

28-September-2025

Today, dear Libra, focus on self-care. You've been giving a lot of yourself lately, and now it's time to nurture your mind, body, and spirit. Taking time to rest and recharge will restore your energy and bring balance back into your life.

Affirmation & Gratitude

"I honor my body, mind, and spirit by prioritizing self-care and rest."

Libra

29-September-2025

Today, dear Libra, expect the unexpected. A surprise opportunity or change may arise, so stay flexible and open to possibilities. Trust that these shifts are leading you toward growth and positive transformation.

Affirmation & Gratitude

"I welcome unexpected changes, trusting that they bring growth and positive transformation into my life."

Libra

30-September-2025

Today, dear Libra, reflection is key. Take a moment to look back at your progress this month and celebrate your accomplishments, big and small. Use this time to set new intentions for the future and embrace the growth you've achieved.

Affirmation & Gratitude

"I honor my progress and celebrate my journey, trusting that I am always growing and evolving."

October 2025

Libra
01-October-2025

Today, dear Libra, the new month brings fresh opportunities. Focus on setting your intentions and aligning yourself with your goals. The energy of new beginnings will propel you toward exciting possibilities, so embrace the change.

Affirmation & Gratitude

"I welcome the new month with optimism, setting clear intentions for growth and success."

Libra
02-October-2025

Today, dear Libra, balance is key. You may feel stretched thin by various responsibilities, but with organization and self-care, you will maintain harmony. Don't hesitate to set boundaries where needed.

Affirmation & Gratitude

"I create balance in my life by setting healthy boundaries and honoring my needs."

Libra
03-October-2025

Today, dear Libra, focus on communication. Clear and open conversations will help resolve any lingering issues, bringing peace and understanding to your relationships. Speak your truth with kindness and listen deeply to others.

Affirmation & Gratitude

"I communicate with clarity and kindness, fostering harmony in all my relationships."

Libra

04-October-2025

Today, dear Libra, your creativity is flowing. Whether you're starting a new project or solving a problem, let your imagination guide you. Trust that your ideas have value and that they can lead to exciting new opportunities.

Affirmation & Gratitude

"I trust my creativity to guide me toward fresh ideas and exciting possibilities."

Libra
05-October-2025

Today, dear Libra, relationships are in focus. Nurture your connections by spending quality time with loved ones and showing appreciation. Small acts of kindness will go a long way in strengthening your bonds and bringing joy to your day.

Affirmation & Gratitude

"I nurture my relationships with love and attention, building deeper connections with those I care about."

Libra

06-October-2025

Today, dear Libra, it's time for self-reflection. Take a step back from the hustle and spend some quiet time alone. Meditation or journaling will help you gain clarity on your thoughts and emotions, guiding you toward peace.

Affirmation & Gratitude

"I connect with my inner self, allowing peace and clarity to guide my path."

Libra
07-October-2025

Today, dear Libra, focus on personal growth. Take steps to improve yourself, whether through learning a new skill or working on self-awareness. Every effort you make will bring you closer to becoming the best version of yourself.

Affirmation & Gratitude

"I embrace opportunities for personal growth, knowing that every step brings me closer to my highest potential."

Libra
08-October-2025

Today, dear Libra, financial matters may need attention. Review your budget, savings, or investments, and make adjustments where necessary. Thoughtful planning today will bring future abundance and security.

Affirmation & Gratitude

"I make wise financial decisions that ensure my long-term security and prosperity."

Libra

09-October-2025

Today, dear Libra, adventure calls! Step out of your routine and embrace something new, whether it's a trip, hobby, or a spontaneous activity. Embracing the unknown will bring excitement and open the door to growth.

Affirmation & Gratitude

"I welcome new adventures into my life, trusting that they bring joy and growth."

Libra
10-October-2025

Today, dear Libra, emotions may run high. Take time to process your feelings and approach any conflicts with compassion. Vulnerability can lead to deeper understanding and healing, so allow yourself to feel and express your emotions.

Affirmation & Gratitude

"I embrace my emotions with kindness, allowing them to guide me toward healing and connection."

Libra
11-October-2025

Today, dear Libra, focus on relationships. Strengthen your connections by being present and showing appreciation for those around you. Small gestures of kindness and thoughtful conversations will deepen your bonds.

Affirmation & Gratitude

"I nurture my relationships with love, building deeper connections with those I cherish."

Libra

12-October-2025

Today, dear Libra, financial planning is in focus. Review your goals and make adjustments where necessary to align with your long-term vision. Wise decisions made today will lead to future security and abundance.

Affirmation & Gratitude

"I make thoughtful financial choices that support my long-term stability and success."

Libra

13-October-2025

Today, dear Libra, your creativity is at its peak. Use this energy to brainstorm new ideas or take action on a creative project. Your innovative thinking will lead you toward fresh solutions and exciting possibilities.

Affirmation & Gratitude

"I trust my creative energy to guide me toward new ideas and exciting opportunities."

Libra
14-October-2025

Today, dear Libra, focus on gratitude. Take time to reflect on the blessings in your life and express appreciation for them. Gratitude will attract even more joy and abundance into your world.

Affirmation & Gratitude

"I am grateful for the blessings in my life, and I welcome even more abundance with an open heart."

Libra
15-October-2025

Today, dear Libra, balance is essential. You may feel torn between various obligations, but prioritizing self-care will help you stay centered. Don't be afraid to say no where necessary to protect your energy.

Affirmation & Gratitude

"I create balance in my life by prioritizing my wellbeing and setting healthy boundaries."

Libra
16-October-2025

Today, dear Libra, relationships are highlighted. Meaningful conversations and shared moments will bring you closer to loved ones. Show appreciation and nurture the connections that matter most to you.

Affirmation & Gratitude

"I nurture my relationships with love and attention, strengthening the bonds that matter most."

Libra

17-October-2025

Today, dear Libra, creativity flows easily. Use this energy to explore new ideas or dive into a creative project. Your imagination is your greatest asset today, so trust in your ability to innovate and create something special.

Affirmation & Gratitude

"I embrace my creativity and trust in my ability to bring fresh ideas to life."

Libra
18-October-2025

Today, dear Libra, focus on collaboration. Working with others will lead to greater success, whether in professional or personal endeavors. Appreciate the unique strengths of those around you, and trust in the power of teamwork.

Affirmation & Gratitude

"I embrace the power of teamwork, knowing that collaboration leads to greater success and fulfillment."

Libra
19-October-2025

Today, dear Libra, adventure awaits. Step out of your comfort zone and try something new, whether it's a spontaneous trip or learning a new skill. Embracing new experiences will lead to growth and joy.

Affirmation & Gratitude

"I welcome new adventures, trusting that they bring joy and personal growth."

Libra

20-October-2025

Today, dear Libra, emotions may surface. Take time to process your feelings and approach any conflicts with compassion. By allowing yourself to be vulnerable, you'll strengthen your connections and foster deeper understanding.

Affirmation & Gratitude

"I embrace my emotions with kindness, allowing them to guide me toward healing and deeper connections."

Libra

21-October-2025

Today, dear Libra, focus on personal growth. Take steps to improve yourself, whether through learning something new or deepening your self-awareness. Every small effort contributes to your transformation.

Affirmation & Gratitude

"I embrace opportunities for personal growth, knowing that each step brings me closer to my true potential."

Libra
22-October-2025

Today, dear Libra, communication is key. Clear, honest conversations will resolve any misunderstandings and create harmony in your relationships. Speak your truth with kindness, and listen with an open heart.

Affirmation & Gratitude

"I communicate with clarity and kindness, fostering understanding and harmony in all my interactions."

Libra

23-October-2025

Today, dear Libra, focus on self-care. You've been giving a lot of yourself lately, and now it's time to recharge. Whether through relaxation, pampering, or simply taking a break, nurturing yourself will restore your energy and bring balance.

Affirmation & Gratitude

"I honor myself by taking time to rest and recharge, knowing I deserve love and care."

Libra

24-October-2025

Today, dear Libra, creativity flows effortlessly. Use this energy to explore new projects or brainstorm fresh ideas. Trust that your creative spark will lead you toward exciting opportunities and innovations.

Affirmation & Gratitude

"I celebrate my creativity and trust my ability to bring new ideas to life."

Libra

25-October-2025

Today, dear Libra, relationships are in focus. Nurture your connections through meaningful conversations and shared experiences. Small acts of kindness will strengthen your bonds and bring more joy into your day.

Affirmation & Gratitude

"I nurture my relationships with love and care, building deeper connections with those I cherish."

Libra

26-October-2025

Today, dear Libra, financial matters may require attention. Take time to review your budget or long-term plans, and make adjustments if needed. Thoughtful planning today will lead to future stability and abundance.

Affirmation & Gratitude

"I make wise financial decisions that support my long-term security and prosperity."

Libra
27-October-2025

Today, dear Libra, focus on gratitude. Reflect on the blessings in your life and express appreciation for them. Gratitude will attract even more abundance and joy into your world, filling your heart with happiness.

Affirmation & Gratitude

"I am grateful for the blessings in my life, and I welcome even more joy and abundance with an open heart."

Libra

28-October-2025

Today, dear Libra, creativity is your guiding light. Let your imagination flow freely, and use it to solve problems or create something new. Your innovative ideas will lead you toward exciting opportunities.

Affirmation & Gratitude

"I trust my creative energy to guide me toward new ideas and exciting possibilities."

Libra
29-October-2025

Today, dear Libra, emotions may run high. Take time to ground yourself and process your feelings before reacting. Approach any conflicts with compassion and understanding, and allow your emotions to guide you toward healing.

Affirmation & Gratitude

"I embrace my emotions with kindness, allowing them to guide me toward healing and deeper understanding."

Libra
30-October-2025

Today, dear Libra, relationships take center stage. Show your loved ones how much you appreciate them through thoughtful conversations and small gestures of kindness. Building deeper connections will bring more harmony into your life.

Affirmation & Gratitude

"I nurture my relationships with love and attention, building deeper bonds with those I care about."

Libra

31-October-2025

Today, dear Libra, reflection is key. As the month ends, take time to look back on your progress and celebrate your accomplishments. Use this reflective energy to set new goals for the coming month, embracing all the growth you've achieved.

Affirmation & Gratitude

"I honor my progress and celebrate my journey, trusting that I am always growing and evolving."

November 2025

Libra

01-November-2025

Today, dear Libra, fresh energy surrounds you. Set your intentions for the new month and align your goals with your inner desires. This is a powerful time to manifest what you want, so stay focused and positive.

Affirmation & Gratitude

"I set clear intentions and trust that the universe supports my dreams and desires."

Libra

02-November-2025

Today, dear Libra, balance is crucial. You may feel overwhelmed by responsibilities, but creating a clear plan and prioritizing self-care will help you stay grounded. Find peace in the small moments of rest.

Affirmation & Gratitude

"I create balance in my life by honoring my needs and setting healthy boundaries."

Libra

03-November-2025

Today, dear Libra, communication flows smoothly. It's a great day to clear up misunderstandings or have deep conversations with loved ones. Your words have the power to heal, so speak with kindness and intention.

Affirmation & Gratitude

"I communicate openly and honestly, fostering harmony in my relationships."

Libra

04-November-2025

Today, dear Libra, creativity is abundant. Use this energy to work on a passion project, start a new hobby, or solve problems creatively. Your imagination will lead you toward exciting and fresh ideas.

Affirmation & Gratitude

"I embrace my creative energy and allow it to guide me toward new possibilities."

Libra

05-November-2025

Today, dear Libra, focus on relationships. Whether romantic, familial, or friendships, nurturing your connections through kindness and understanding will bring harmony and joy. Be present with those who matter most to you.

Affirmation & Gratitude

"I nurture my relationships with love and compassion, creating deeper bonds with those I cherish."

Libra

06-November-2025

Today, dear Libra, self-care is essential. You've been giving a lot of yourself recently, and now it's time to recharge. Prioritize rest and relaxation to restore your energy and bring balance back into your life.

Affirmation & Gratitude

"I honor my mind, body, and spirit by taking time to rest and recharge."

Libra

07-November-2025

Today, dear Libra, focus on financial planning. Review your budget or investments and make adjustments where needed. Practical decisions made today will lead to long-term stability and peace of mind.

Affirmation & Gratitude

"I make wise financial choices that support my long-term security and prosperity."

Libra

08-November-2025

Today, dear Libra, expect the unexpected. A surprise opportunity may present itself, so stay open and flexible. Trust that changes happening now are guiding you toward growth and positive transformation.

Affirmation & Gratitude

"I welcome unexpected opportunities, trusting that they bring growth and positive change into my life."

Libra

09-November-2025

Today, dear Libra, emotions may run high. Take time to reflect on your feelings and approach any conflicts with compassion. Vulnerability leads to healing, so don't shy away from expressing your emotions.

Affirmation & Gratitude

"I embrace my emotions with kindness, allowing them to guide me toward healing and deeper understanding."

Libra

10-November-2025

Today, dear Libra, your social side shines. Reconnect with friends or family, and enjoy lighthearted conversations. Laughter and shared moments will bring joy and strengthen your connections, leaving you feeling uplifted.

Affirmation & Gratitude

"I cherish my relationships and enjoy the joy and connection they bring into my life."

Libra

11-November-2025

Today, dear Libra, focus on long-term goals. Take time to reassess your plans and make necessary adjustments. Consistency and dedication will lead to success, so stay focused and trust the process.

Affirmation & Gratitude

"I set clear goals and take consistent steps toward achieving them, trusting in my ability to succeed."

Libra

12-November-2025

Today, dear Libra, creativity flows effortlessly. Let your imagination guide you, whether through artistic projects or finding innovative solutions. Trust that your ideas have value, and allow your creative energy to lead the way.

Affirmation & Gratitude

"I trust my creativity to guide me toward new ideas and exciting possibilities."

Libra

13-November-2025

Today, dear Libra, balance is key. You may feel pulled in different directions, but prioritizing your wellbeing will help you maintain harmony. Don't hesitate to set boundaries and take time for self-care when needed.

Affirmation & Gratitude

"I create balance in my life by setting healthy boundaries and prioritizing my needs."

Libra
14-November-2025

Today, dear Libra, relationships are highlighted. Spend quality time with loved ones, and deepen your connections through meaningful conversations. Acts of kindness and understanding will bring harmony into your relationships.

Affirmation & Gratitude

"I nurture my relationships with love and care, building deeper connections with those I cherish."

Libra

15-November-2025

Today, dear Libra, financial matters may require attention. Review your budget or make necessary adjustments to your long-term financial plans. Thoughtful planning today will ensure future security and abundance.

Affirmation & Gratitude

"I make wise financial choices that lead to security and prosperity in the long run."

Libra
16-November-2025

Today, dear Libra, focus on self-reflection. Quiet moments of introspection will help you gain clarity on your thoughts and emotions. Journaling, meditation, or time in nature will allow you to connect deeply with your inner self.

Affirmation & Gratitude

"I connect with my inner wisdom, trusting that it guides me toward clarity and peace."

Libra

17-November-2025

Today, dear Libra, collaboration will bring success. Whether in work or personal projects, working with others will lead to greater results. Appreciate the unique strengths of your team, and trust in the power of collective effort.

Affirmation & Gratitude

"I embrace the power of teamwork, knowing that collaboration leads to greater success and fulfillment."

Libra

18-November-2025

Today, dear Libra, adventure calls. Step outside your comfort zone and embrace something new, whether it's a new hobby, place, or experience. Embracing new adventures will bring excitement and opportunities for growth.

Affirmation & Gratitude

"I welcome new adventures, trusting that they bring joy and personal growth."

Libra
19-November-2025

Today, dear Libra, emotions may surface. Take time to process your feelings and approach conflicts with compassion. Vulnerability will strengthen your connections, so allow yourself to be open and honest with those you trust.

Affirmation & Gratitude

"I embrace my emotions with kindness, allowing them to guide me toward healing and deeper connections."

Libra

20-November-2025

Today, dear Libra, creativity is abundant. Whether through art, writing, or problem-solving, let your imagination flow freely. Your creative energy will lead you toward fresh ideas and exciting possibilities.

Affirmation & Gratitude

"I celebrate my creativity and trust in my ability to bring fresh ideas to life."

Libra

21-November-2025

Today, dear Libra, focus on financial security. Take time to review your savings or investments, and make thoughtful decisions for the future. Practical planning today will lead to long-term abundance and peace of mind.

Affirmation & Gratitude

"I make wise financial decisions that support my long-term stability and prosperity."

Libra

22-November-2025

Today, dear Libra, relationships take center stage. Spend quality time with loved ones, and show appreciation for those who support you. Small gestures of kindness and thoughtful conversations will deepen your bonds.

Affirmation & Gratitude

"I nurture my relationships with love and care, creating deeper connections with those I cherish."

Libra

23-November-2025

Today, dear Libra, communication is key. Honest conversations will help resolve misunderstandings and strengthen your relationships. Speak from the heart, and listen with empathy to create harmony in your interactions.

Affirmation & Gratitude

"I communicate with clarity and kindness, fostering understanding in all my relationships."

Libra

24-November-2025

Today, dear Libra, focus on self-care. You've been giving a lot of yourself lately, and now it's time to recharge. Whether through relaxation, mindfulness, or spending time in nature, nurturing yourself will restore your energy and balance.

Affirmation & Gratitude

"I honor myself by taking time to rest and recharge, knowing I deserve love and care."

Libra

25-November-2025

Today, dear Libra, new opportunities may arise. Stay open to possibilities that may seem unexpected or unconventional. Embracing change with confidence will lead to exciting growth and positive transformation.

Affirmation & Gratitude

"I welcome new opportunities with an open heart, trusting that they bring growth and success."

Libra

26-November-2025

Today, dear Libra, emotions may be intense. Ground yourself by spending time in quiet reflection or meditation. Allow your emotions to guide you toward healing, and approach any conflicts with compassion and understanding.

Affirmation & Gratitude

"I embrace my emotions with compassion, allowing them to guide me toward healing and peace."

Libra

27-November-2025

Today, dear Libra, focus on adventure. Break away from your routine and try something new, whether it's travel, a new hobby, or exploring a new idea. Embracing the unknown will bring excitement and personal growth.

Affirmation & Gratitude

"I welcome new adventures into my life, trusting that they bring joy and expansion."

Libra

28-November-2025

Today, dear Libra, creativity is your greatest ally. Let your imagination flow freely and use it to solve problems or create something new. Trust in your ability to innovate, and watch as fresh opportunities unfold.

Affirmation & Gratitude

"I trust my creativity to guide me toward new ideas and exciting possibilities."

Libra

29-November-2025

Today, dear Libra, focus on balance. With various demands on your time, it's essential to maintain harmony within. Set boundaries where needed, and prioritize both work and relaxation to keep yourself centered.

Affirmation & Gratitude

"I create balance in my life by setting boundaries and honoring my need for rest."

Libra

30-November-2025

Today, dear Libra, reflection is key. As the month ends, take time to look back on your progress and celebrate your accomplishments. Set new intentions for the coming month, and embrace the growth you've achieved.

Affirmation & Gratitude

"I celebrate my progress and set new intentions for growth, trusting that I am always evolving."

December 2025

Libra

01-December-2025

Today, dear Libra, fresh beginnings surround you. As the last month of the year begins, set your intentions for growth and joy. This is a time to reflect on your journey and embrace the opportunities ahead.

Affirmation & Gratitude

"I welcome December with open arms, setting intentions for joy, growth, and peace."

Libra

02-December-2025

Today, dear Libra, balance is key. You may feel pulled in many directions, but staying grounded will help you manage everything with grace. Prioritize your wellbeing, and don't be afraid to delegate where needed.

Affirmation & Gratitude

"I maintain balance by prioritizing my wellbeing and setting boundaries when necessary."

Libra
03-December-2025

Today, dear Libra, communication is essential. Clear, honest conversations will strengthen your relationships and resolve any lingering misunderstandings. Speak with kindness, and listen with empathy to foster deeper connections.

Affirmation & Gratitude

"I communicate openly and with kindness, fostering understanding and harmony in all my relationships."

Libra
04-December-2025

Today, dear Libra, creativity flows effortlessly. Let your imagination run free and dive into a new project or explore innovative ideas. Your creative energy will lead you toward exciting possibilities and new beginnings.

Affirmation & Gratitude

"I trust my creativity to guide me toward fresh ideas and exciting opportunities."

Libra

05-December-2025

Today, dear Libra, focus on relationships. Nurture your connections with love and attention, showing appreciation for those around you. Thoughtful gestures will deepen your bonds and bring more harmony into your day.

Affirmation & Gratitude

"I nurture my relationships with love and care, creating deeper connections with those I cherish."

Libra

06-December-2025

Today, dear Libra, it's time for self-care. You've been giving a lot of yourself recently, and now it's time to recharge. Whether through rest, relaxation, or simply taking time for yourself, prioritize your wellbeing today.

Affirmation & Gratitude

"I honor my body, mind, and spirit by taking time to rest and recharge."

Libra
07-December-2025

Today, dear Libra, financial matters may require your attention. Take time to review your budget or long-term plans, and make adjustments where needed. Practical planning today will ensure future security and abundance.

Affirmation & Gratitude

"I make wise financial decisions that support my long-term security and prosperity."

Libra

08-December-2025

Today, dear Libra, emotions may surface. Allow yourself to feel deeply and process your emotions with compassion. Approach conflicts with kindness and understanding, knowing that vulnerability can lead to healing.

Affirmation & Gratitude

"I embrace my emotions with kindness, allowing them to guide me toward healing and deeper connections."

Libra
09-December-2025

Today, dear Libra, adventure calls! Step outside your comfort zone and explore new experiences, whether it's travel, a new hobby, or meeting new people. Embracing the unknown will bring excitement and joy.

Affirmation & Gratitude

"I welcome new adventures into my life, trusting that they bring joy and growth."

Libra

10-December-2025

Today, dear Libra, focus on collaboration. Working with others will lead to success, whether in personal or professional endeavors. Appreciate the strengths of those around you, and trust that teamwork will bring greater results.

Affirmation & Gratitude

"I embrace the power of teamwork, knowing that collaboration leads to greater success."

Libra

11-December-2025

Today, dear Libra, creativity is abundant. Use this energy to brainstorm new ideas or start a new project. Trust in your ability to innovate, and let your imagination guide you toward fresh opportunities and exciting ventures.

Affirmation & Gratitude

"I trust my creativity to bring fresh ideas and new opportunities into my life."

Libra
12-December-2025

Today, dear Libra, balance is important. You may feel torn between responsibilities, but prioritizing your self-care will help you stay grounded. Don't be afraid to set boundaries and protect your energy where needed.

Affirmation & Gratitude

"I create balance in my life by prioritizing my wellbeing and setting healthy boundaries."

Libra

13-December-2025

Today, dear Libra, focus on relationships. Spend quality time with loved ones, and show appreciation for their support. Meaningful conversations and small acts of kindness will strengthen your bonds and bring harmony into your relationships.

Affirmation & Gratitude

"I nurture my relationships with love and care, creating deeper connections with those I cherish."

Libra

14-December-2025

Today, dear Libra, financial planning is key. Take a closer look at your long-term goals and make necessary adjustments to your budget or investments. Practical decisions today will lead to future security and abundance.

Affirmation & Gratitude

"I make wise financial choices that support my long-term prosperity and peace of mind."

Libra
15-December-2025

Today, dear Libra, emotions may be intense. Take time to reflect on your feelings and approach any conflicts with compassion. Vulnerability and honesty will deepen your connections and bring healing where needed.

Affirmation & Gratitude

"I embrace my emotions with compassion, allowing them to guide me toward healing and understanding."

Libra

16-December-2025

Today, dear Libra, focus on creativity. Whether it's art, writing, or problem-solving, let your imagination guide you. Your creative energy will lead to new solutions and exciting opportunities for personal and professional growth.

Affirmation & Gratitude

"I celebrate my creativity and trust my ability to bring new ideas to life."

Libra

17-December-2025

Today, dear Libra, collaboration is key. Working with others will bring greater success than working alone. Appreciate the unique strengths of those around you, and trust that teamwork will lead to exciting results.

Affirmation & Gratitude

"I embrace the power of teamwork, knowing that collaboration leads to greater success and fulfillment."

Libra

18-December-2025

Today, dear Libra, gratitude is your guiding light. Take time to reflect on the blessings in your life and express appreciation for them. Gratitude will attract even more abundance and joy into your world.

Affirmation & Gratitude

"I am grateful for the blessings in my life, and I welcome even more abundance with an open heart."

Libra
19-December-2025

Today, dear Libra, focus on self-care. You've been working hard, and now it's time to rest and recharge. Pampering yourself with love and care will restore your energy and help you feel more centered.

Affirmation & Gratitude

"I honor myself by taking time to rest and recharge, knowing I deserve love and care."

Libra
20-December-2025

Today, dear Libra, creativity flows effortlessly. Use this energy to explore new ideas, start a personal project, or find innovative solutions. Your imagination is your greatest asset today, so let it guide you toward exciting possibilities.

Affirmation & Gratitude

"I trust my creativity to bring fresh ideas and exciting opportunities into my life."

Libra

21-December-2025

Today, dear Libra, focus on relationships. Meaningful conversations and shared experiences will bring you closer to loved ones. Show appreciation for those who support you, and deepen your bonds through love and kindness.

Affirmation & Gratitude

"I nurture my relationships with love, creating deeper connections with those I cherish."

Libra

22-December-2025

Today, dear Libra, balance is essential. With various responsibilities pulling at you, it's important to prioritize both work and relaxation. Set boundaries where needed to protect your energy, and make time for yourself.

Affirmation & Gratitude

"I maintain balance in my life by setting healthy boundaries and honoring my need for rest."

Libra

23-December-2025

Today, dear Libra, emotions may be intense. Take time to process your feelings and approach any conflicts with compassion. Vulnerability will lead to healing and deeper understanding, so allow yourself to feel and express your emotions.

Affirmation & Gratitude

"I embrace my emotions with kindness, allowing them to guide me toward healing and deeper understanding."

Libra

24-December-2025

Today, dear Libra, focus on gratitude. Reflect on the blessings in your life, and express appreciation for them. Gratitude will attract even more abundance and joy into your world, filling your heart with happiness.

Affirmation & Gratitude

"I am grateful for the blessings in my life, and I welcome even more joy and abundance with an open heart."

Libra
25-December-2025

Today, dear Libra, nurture your relationships. The love and care you show to others will create harmony in your interactions. Take time to celebrate and cherish the connections you've built with those who matter most.

Affirmation & Gratitude

"I nurture my relationships with love and attention, creating deeper bonds with those I cherish."

Libra

26-December-2025

Today, dear Libra, focus on adventure. Break away from your routine and embrace new experiences, whether through travel, a new hobby, or spontaneous activities. Embracing the unknown will bring excitement and growth.

Affirmation & Gratitude

"I welcome new adventures into my life, trusting that they bring joy and growth."

Libra

27-December-2025

Today, dear Libra, collaboration will lead to success. Working with others will bring fresh perspectives and greater results than working alone. Trust in the power of teamwork and appreciate the strengths of those around you.

Affirmation & Gratitude

"I embrace the power of teamwork, knowing that collaboration brings greater success and fulfillment."

Libra
28-December-2025

Today, dear Libra, emotions may be heightened. Take time to ground yourself through meditation, reflection, or a walk in nature. Allow your emotions to guide you toward healing and deeper understanding.

Affirmation & Gratitude

"I embrace my emotions with compassion, allowing them to guide me toward healing and peace."

Libra
29-December-2025

Today, dear Libra, focus on self-care. You've been giving a lot of yourself lately, and now it's time to nurture your mind, body, and spirit. Small acts of kindness toward yourself will go a long way in restoring balance and joy.

Affirmation & Gratitude

"I honor myself by prioritizing self-care, knowing that I deserve love, kindness, and rest."

Libra

30-December-2025

Today, dear Libra, creativity is your greatest asset. Whether you're working on a personal project or solving a problem, trust your imagination to lead you toward new ideas and exciting opportunities.

Affirmation & Gratitude

"I trust my creativity to bring fresh ideas and exciting possibilities into my life."

Libra

31-December-2025

Today, dear Libra, reflect on your journey as the year comes to a close. Celebrate your accomplishments and growth, and set new intentions for the coming year. Embrace the excitement of what's to come and all you've achieved.

Affirmation & Gratitude

"I celebrate my growth and set new intentions for the year ahead, welcoming new opportunities and possibilities."

The Answers You Seek

Are Within

The "Daily Guidance" series offers an innovative approach to finding spiritual wisdom and practical advice. Each book in the series is a unique tool designed for daily introspection and decision-making. Readers are invited to meditate on a question or seek general guidance for the day, then flip to a random page in the book. The page they land on provides a personalized message from various spiritual sources, such as angels, tarot, or spirit animals. With each turn of the page, these books deliver insightful, positive messages and mantras to inspire personal growth and provide clarity on life's daily challenges and decisions.

Other books in this series:-
The Angelic Oracles
Daily Angel Tarot Reading
Mystic Tarot Cat
Oracle of the Tarot Cat
Vibes Unveiled
Spirit Animal Oracle
Answers from the Oracles
Messages from the Angels

Daily Guidance
SERIES

More on the Bookshelves at
www.korupublishing.com

www.ingramcontent.com/pod-product-compliance
Ingram Content Group UK Ltd.
Pitfield, Milton Keynes, MK11 3LW, UK
UKHW020956040225
4424UKWH00037B/167

9 781763 623750